I0091458

Blinded by Color

Amanda J Scoby

© Copyright 2021 - Amanda J Scoby

All Rights Reserved.

ISBN: 978-0-578-89295-5

No part of this book may be reproduced or transmitted in any form or by any means; graphic, electronic, or mechanical, including photocopying, recording, taping or by any information storage retrieval system without written permission of the author.

Printed in the United States of America

1

Kayla

I woke up to a message alert, causing my phone to beep repeatedly until I checked it. The noise alone can drive you insane. It was my best friend, Nivea. Niv, as I like to call her, is always sending me things from Facebook. She thinks that if she finds it interesting, well, then everyone else must agree. Niv and I have been best friends for as long as I can remember. She is not your average girl. Niv is bold and has no fear. She does not redeem the name ladylike when people describe her. In fact, Niv is like one of the guys. She stands at a whopping five feet on her best day, but her attitude is about seven feet tall. She is loud and never avoids confrontation. The girl is a beast. She probably weighs around 125, but every inch of her is muscle. Niv loves sports. She is a fighter and never backs down from a dare. She is the kind of friend people spend a lifetime looking to claim. I got lucky; we met in grade school. Growing up here in Lutz, just outside of Tampa, things are slow-paced, and it's a beach town lifestyle. We take bike rides and spend evenings having barbeques and laughing around a bonfire on the beach. We like to swim or surf and rollerblade around our neighborhood. With all that being said, we are not rich. Tampa is not the richest of areas. Small houses made of concrete for the hot weather and lots of windows. It is humid, and that means as little clothes as possible. My house is in a cul-de-sac on the corner of Tin Smith Circle. Niv lives two streets over and always has. My mom is also friends with Niv's mom. They like to hang out and talk crap out back or at the bar. The locals always go to the same bar, The Basement! My mom is well known around town and not in a good way. She is your local drunk, loud, and obnoxious. The town sheriff brings her home most nights. I guess I should add the local sheriff is my mom's brother, my uncle Rodney.

Sometimes I wonder how different my life would have been if my dad had not died. He passed when I was just ten years old. I would give anything to remember him more and see him one last time. The thing is, my dad was murdered, and his murder has never been solved. This was the turning point for my mom. This was when she became a drunk, drinking away her feelings. Joanna, or Slim as they like to call her for her small frame and tiny features, is not a Betty Crocker, to say the least. She has never remarried or dated another man after my father's death. I do believe a lot of one-night stands have taken place, but I will never know for sure.

I hear the alert again! BLOOP! I am going to have to change that one day. The message reads, "New Testing Reveals False DNA Results." The article is long and uninteresting to me, but to be fair, I click on the link to amuse myself while lying in my bed. I know it will be hot outside, and I am too tired to jump up and get ready. I just want to remain in my bed and self-loath. I roll over on my stomach and begin scrolling down through the article, trying to catch enough of the facts that I can pretend I read it when I see Niv and she excitedly asks what I thought. The article is about those DNA kits you can purchase where you spit in a tube and find out your history. I have zero interest in this, but if it made the news and there could be a conspiracy, you could bet Niv was interested. I skim it over and decide I gathered enough information to make it seem real that I cared. I back out of the messages and click on my feed. I am surprised to see a picture of my ex pop up with a new girl next to him. The cold hard facts hit me like a ton of bricks. Under the picture, it reads, "Why would I jump out the car for a penny when I am riding with a dime," and I thought, wow, he never even posted a pic of me! What makes her so special? I am not at all jealous, but I am offended. I also do not recognize this girl, so she must be from out of town. Now my curiosity has peaked, and I am dying to know where she is from. She looks like trailer trash to me. My first guess – she is from the wrong side of the tracks. Her teeth look brown, and I assume she smokes. Her lips are cracked like she's in need of Chapstick, and her roots are black with blonde ends. I can only guess she colors her own hair, and she clearly does not do it well since I see several orange spots all over her head. This photo could not look any worse. She is covered in tattoos. Lots of skulls and a full sleeve. I am baffled by what he could possibly see in her. She has terrible acne on her face, especially on her chin and forehead. Her hair looks greasy like she never washes it, and she is wearing what used to be a white tank top, I presume, but it has now faded to gray. She is a thicker girl and has a huge chest with bigger arms and a pudgy stomach. They are sitting down together in the picture, and her jeans are dirty, and she has rolls hanging out of her shirt. I am so confused why he would post this photo and think it was a perfect shot. If this is the best she looks, then I feel sorry for him and her. However, my curiosity told me to click on her name since he tagged her in the photo so I could get the 411. I read the name and repeated it out loud and decided not to do it. That name, though – Jessica The Realist. Why did she feel the need to use a name like that over her real name? I hated when people decided to name themselves with a title like they were a headline. Ugh! I threw my phone to the end of the bed and grabbed my pillow and shoved my face in it while I screamed at the top of my lungs. I felt the burning in my eyes like tears were about to fall, and then I caved. The tears came pouring out, and I felt sick.

My ex, otherwise known as Josh, was a total jerk nine-ty-nine percent of the time. That was just who he was and how he executed his thoughts, but I saw potential. He was smart and drove a black 3 series BMW to prove it. He quoted movies like he was in them. He was an intellectual, and he had his own place. A small apartment above a barbershop, but it suited him. He had nice furniture, and he was within walking distance to the beach. He worked selling Ad space for a small agency, but he always met his quota and got the bonus checks to splurge. He spoiled me, and I loved it. When he wanted to, he could be the sweetest guy you ever met, but when he was talking, it was mostly arrogance that took over. His mouth would never catch up to his brain. You know the part that says, *stop, do not say that*. He did not care if he hurt feelings. He did not even care if you liked him. He knew he was a good catch and that after being on the wrestling team and competing nationally, he retained his physique. He was fit and tall with beautiful green eyes! Blonde hair, like a true surf-er and that sun-kissed tan people pay big money for. He was beautiful. He dressed like he made millions, and he smelled amazing. I couldn't see us lasting through to forever because his cocky no-nonsense attitude made me hate him. However, I think Miss "Jessica The Realist" probably plays his game very well. She more than likely gasses him up and makes him feel like the big man on campus. I can honestly say this is not sur-prising seeing her in the pic; he is probably everything she ever dreamed of in a man and knew she could never get. Meeting him was like winning the lottery, and she is not going to let go of that ticket.

∼

BOOM! The front door to our small house slammed so loud I knew it could be none other than Nivea coming in to wake me up and talk about Josh. No doubt she saw the photo and cannot wait to see my reaction. Time to play cool because I have 2.5 seconds before…and here she is now in front of me on my bed, out of breath and dying to hear my thoughts.

"Girl, omigosh, did you see Facebook this morning? No, really, like you have to see it! Just hang on, wait till I show you what popped up on my page. Holy hell, Kayla, you are going to die. Literally die! Geeeeesh, my fingers won't go fast enough, and it is taking forever to load."

I sit staring at her while she frantically tries to pull up the photo of Josh and his new fling because why else would she come running to my house. I already know Niv woke up to the picture, and before she even brushed her teeth, she had to come see me to tell me all about it. See, this is the thing about Niv; she is a stylist. We graduated about four years ago from Steinbrenner High School, and Niv is the town cosmetologist. She hears gossip from everywhere. She was sure she was going to be a hairdresser during our junior year. She attended school at the local Votech half the day and attended regular high school for her credits the other half. By the time we graduated, she had started a Facebook fan page and posted so many pics of her work that she blew up. Her abundance of clients made it so Niv could buy a car and pay for it on her own. She wasn't dumb. She made it happen, but in the midst of all that, she became even worse at gossiping. It's like as soon as someone sits in the chair, they open up like this is therapy 101. She knows way too much about way too many people. When I see her, it all comes out like word vomit. There are many times I have to say Niv, "I really don't care what Stephanie is doing and who she is having an affair with," but for Niv, she lives for this kind of drama and the fact that she knows it, well, you might as well have told her she was Oprah.

"Niv, if this is about Josh, I saw it! No need to pull it up." And just like that, she looks up to meet my eyes for the first time since she entered the room and waits with her mouth open wide, looking for my reaction. "Niv, I know you're dying to hear me freak out, but I am not going to do that. Frankly, I don't care. Josh and I are not together anymore, and he can do what he wants. I am happy for him." I was hoping she bought this because I was trying my best to sound convincing, but the thing about Niv is, she knows me like the back of her hand. I cannot lie to her.

"Bullshit! Seriously! Bullshit!"

"I am for real, Niv."

"You can say whatever you want to other people, but let's not forget I know you, girl, and I know you saw this pic and you took one look at that girl and thought all kinds of bad words to call her because I know you, Kayla. I know you need to hide it, but it's okay. I said all the bad words for you, and I don't care who hears it."

Okay, this was my typical Niv. She knows me, and she will call me out.

"Niv, I was sad, but before I could even process it, you came bursting through my door like a whirlwind of disaster. I didn't know if I could even begin to think from how loud you slammed my door."

"Well, in my defense, Josh is dating a hoe from Miami, and not the good part of Miami. She is straight-up Miami trash."

"Okay, first of all, how do you know where she is from?"

I clicked on her name.

"Look, I'll show you, her page isn't even private."

And there it was, all the pictures and proof I needed. A girl from the Miami Dade ghetto who moved up here to Tampa to live with her grandmother and get a fresh start at life. Here I was sitting on my bed with my best friend looking at pictures of my ex's new girlfriend, and I felt the burn again. This time, I couldn't hide it or stop it. The tears fell, and as each one hit my cheek, I felt the waterworks getting stronger, and I knew I was about to lose it. Why does an ex have this effect on you? On anyone. Why do we care? Why does it matter if he was a jerk and you ended it? I ended this horrific spiral a year ago, and here I am, crying on my bed like it was yesterday.

2

Nivea

I walked into my salon and began looking at my appointment book to see who was on my list of victims. I knew I had to be busy since I always was, but I loved to know if I was doing someone I could not stand or someone I loved. You know how it's like; some clients are just the most wonderful people, and you love to see them, and then others you wish would find a new stylist and never come back. As I am scrolling through my computer database to see my book, I notice an unfamiliar name – Miranda Levitt. I look at the name, and I swear it looks familiar, but at this point, I know all my clients, and this one does not ring a bell. I decide to search in my client database to see if I ever did her hair before. I click "enter," and it shows zero results. I check to see how she booked, and it appears she found me online and used my website to book her appointment. I am surprised because when you book online, you input all your information, and it clearly states she lives in Myrtle Beach, SC. Why would she be booking for color and a cut if she lives somewhere else? Surely, she has a stylist. I mean, most people go on vacation and get a blowout or style but never color and a cut.

I start to prep for my first client, Mrs. Eugene Robins. She is elderly and has lived here in Lutz her whole life. She makes me smile and always tells me lovely stories from her upbringing and what changes have occurred over the years. You know those old ladies you just love, the ones with white hair who come to you for a roller set and talk like the world is full of evil because life was bliss in their day. The ones who just hug you and call you sweetie and tell you how good you look. Yup, that's my Mrs. Robins! The grandmother I never had but always wanted. She must be all of eighty now or more, but she still drives herself to the appointments and talks her crap when she wants.

My salon is small; it only holds four stylist chairs, hard wood floors, a small color section for me to mix up formulas, and a washer and dryer room. I have a small storage closet, and of course, hood dryers and shampoo bowls in a line, two each. My color palette for my salon is neutral. I wanted to make sure I did not overdo it like my personality. I chose to go with off whites and tan but added a mint green to brighten it up. My stylist chairs sit across from one another; they are mint-colored leather. My mirrors are surrounded by white rocks and gemstones that sparkle. My hard wood floors compliment my off-white walls; they are ivory like the tusk of an elephant. My bathroom looks like a tan boring khaki-colored room, but it gives the feeling of bougie. My shampoo bowls are white, and I have the walls behind them in floor-to-ceiling mirrors. My salon has huge windows up front when you walk in, and this sunlight adds just the right touch. People love it here. I have designs on my walls in different mint green colors and a touch of gray. It is silhouettes of women and models of big hair. Lots of style, but all me. I am not the type to keep quiet about anything, so I needed a boisterous color to bring about my flare in my shop. This is why, when I found out that Josh had a new girlfriend, I couldn't help but tell Kay. She is my best friend. I had to make sure she knew the asshole she dated, who she claimed to be the most amazing man in the world, was a douche. I never liked the guy. I tried to get her to see that he was rude and arrogant, but she was blinded by love. In this town, you are raised to date the handsome, successful white man. The white-collar man who brings home the bacon. I rebel and take pride in being an independent woman. I like color in my life. This never did fly with Lutz, where everyone is politically challenged. They only see one side, and here, you only bleed red, white, and blue if you are white. However, I built a successful business here. I can't leave. I am from here, and besides, my best friend Kayla, well, she will never leave Lutz. This is her safe haven, and, in my opinion, she will never let go of Josh. My train of thought was interrupted by Mrs.

Robins pushing my salon door open and the bell dinging to let me know someone has entered my shop.

"Good morning, Miss Nivea. It's just me, Mrs. Robins. You are in here somewhere, I'm sure. I'll just be using the ladies' room, you know, old lady problems, honey bun, one day it will be you."

I hear her words smooth as butter on biscuits. God, I love this woman. She just makes me so happy to be alive.

"Good morning, Mrs. Robins," I yell back from my color area. "I will be right up to do your hair."

3

Kayla

I am trying like hell to get ready for work when all I want to do is cry myself to sleep. I hate going to work right now. I hate my life right now. I can't help but wonder what does this girl have that I don't? She is not even his type. Oh, Josh, I just want to text you right now, but every part of me is saying do not do it. Okay, Kay, deep breath, you are fine. I work at a little restaurant in town called the Lutz Diner. I have been working here since I was sixteen, and now at twenty-three years old, I should have moved on, but I can't seem to leave this place. Call it comfort or whatever you want, but I make good money in tips. The owner, Mr. H as we all call him, inherited the diner from his father, and I love the family. Mr. H would do anything for me. I have the schedule I want, I know my regulars who love to sit in my section, and I get free meals. It is a win-win for me. I graduated with my associate's in business management but swore I would get my bachelor's in restaurant management and one day run my own, but those dreams left when I broke up with Josh. I gave up on my future because when you have no one to build it with, it seems less important. I am moving so slow today, putting my hair up in the usual bun, and ironing my uniform, the same one I have worn since I started. The diner does not change much because nothing in this small town does. We do not venture out, and the biggest thing that has ever happened here is my father's unsolved murder. It is the only thing that has ever happened as a major headline in our local paper. People used to whisper and talk about it, but now, it is all a distant memory. For me, it still stings. I am reminded every day when my mom comes home drunk and depressed, slurring her words and swearing. It kills me how much this murder has changed her. She and my father were so in love. They met as kids in high school. My mom only knew my dad, and the same for him. They both graduated the same year and decided to get married and start a family. I was born first, and then my baby brother Jerimiah. Jerimiah is four years younger than me. He still lives at home with Mom and me, but he says he is getting out of here every day. I love him so much, but I swear he keeps secrets from Mom and me. He is always disappearing and leaving for days at a time. I know he is nineteen, but it scares me. He never responds to my texts, and I feel like I lost my dad, my mom, and my brother. Josh was all I had, and now even he is gone.

My mom and dad started off like most couples, poor with just each other to love. They landed a small apartment in Tampa and lived in the city for a few years. My dad worked in a bank. Tampa Financial. He made decent money and worked his way up to branch manager. My mom worked at a gas station as a cashier. Together, they made ends meet. Eventually, when my mom fell pregnant with me, they decided to move back to Lutz and have my dad commute to Tampa. By this time, he was traveling so much for work that we rarely saw him. My mom decided to stay home and tend to me, so I had one active parent in my life. The thing is, my dad was a huge part of my childhood. Every chance he got, he was at my sports events and playing in the yard with me. He was the best dad ever. We always got along. When Jerimiah was born, I was about to start kindergarten, and my mom chose to stay home with him too. She and Jerimiah took to each other like a duck to water. They were super close. He loved dressing up in my mom's clothes and helping her pick out outfits. Jerimiah tried to do the same with me, but I was never interested. I just wanted to hang out with my dad and do father-daughter things. I guess it goes like that in a lot of families, mom and son and father and daughter. Either way, Jerimiah is not close to my mom anymore. He was only six when my dad passed, so he has very little memories of him. At first, my mom's downward spiral was slow, but it quickly picked up, and Jerimiah became my responsibility. For some reason, though, he has really pulled away, and I feel so distant to him. I chalk it up to my mom being a drunk and him losing his best friend and stable relationship, not having a father figure, and hating his sister. I don't know when or why my family had to become so dysfunctional, but I swear it is the never-ending cycle of drama.

～

As I pull up to the diner, I notice the parking lot is full of cars, which means I am going to have a busy day. It's ten minutes to ten, and I am dreading going in, but I know once I do, I will forget all about Josh. I open the door, and I am greeted by Alyssa, my long-time coworker. She is always here; Alyssa loves to pick up shifts and never turns down money. She looks at me with her braces sticking out on her beyond obvious over-bite and says with a mouthful of spit, "It's crazy in here today. I hope you are ready to make some money. It's going to be like this all day." I am stumped for a moment as to why we will be so busy, but then I remember it's wacky Wednesday. Wacky Wednesday is the day Mr. H invented to improve customer morale. He needed to be different. Every Wednesday, we introduce a wacky dish for breakfast, lunch, and dinner. The cooks get super creative, and it looks like today's menu has trumped the rest. I see the chalkboard sign by the hostess stand that reads:

Fresh eggs with grits and marshmallows for added sweetness with mocha pancakes that taste like fresh brewed coffee

Lunch includes our signature catfish and fries with a twisted martini and a spicy watermelon dessert

Dinner is our eel salad for starters with lobster bisque and steak, a side of peppered mashed potatoes and artichoke corn dip

These recipes are always the talk of the town, and Wednesdays bring lots of out-of-towners and Tampa city folks to our little diner. I quickly punch in and tie my apron behind my back. My section is already filling up, and I know I will be crazy busy and super tired by nine pm when my shift ends. I am looking forward to my one-hour lunch break already, and I haven't even started. The good news is, I know the menu by heart, and I could do this job in my sleep, so no matter how much shit I have going on in my life, I can always focus on the task at hand. This is another reason I just can't bring myself to leave this job.

A text pings on my phone just before I go to walk on the floor, so I had to check it. I was secretly hoping it was Josh. The sad truth, though, it was my brother Jerimiah, and his text makes my day even worse.

"Hey, have you heard from mom? I need these college papers signed, and I told her to sign them days ago. She still hasn't, and I can't get an answer from her. Tried several times. Kay, this is serious, Mom needs to sign these papers!"

This is my life; my mom is always somewhere not being a mother, and I am only relevant to my brother when he needs something. I take a second to text back.

"Don't worry, J. I am sure she will show up. If not, sign her name yourself, or I will after work."

4

Jerimiah

"**H**ey sexy, where are you? I noticed you dipped out early this morning."

"Oh, yea, sorry, my love, I have to get these papers signed so we can move and stop hiding our relationship. I am so ready to start our life together."

"Same, I really miss you already though, will I see you tonight?"

"Of course! I love you!"

"Love you more."

I can't stand not being with him anymore. I hate how this family doesn't accept anything other than living the way they deem fit. I am not allowed to date outside my race, I cannot be gay, and my only hope is to be exactly the clone they want me to be. I can't pretend anymore. I am dying on the inside. I feel trapped in my own body, pretending to be this perfect young man who loves women. This young boy who wants to grow up into a man like his father and have children and a successful career. I don't want that life. Since I was a little boy, I loved dressing up in my mom's clothes and pretending to be like her. I am so jealous my sister can wear make-up and no one judges, but she doesn't even take advantage of it. She's just a plain Jane who couldn't care less about her nails or hair. I want to hold hands with this beautiful man who I am dying to marry. I want to be free. I can't take the polluted minds of these suburban white people who think I am supposed to be this heterosexual man. It's not fair. I didn't ask to be born like this. I didn't pray I would be gay. I didn't wake up one day and think, hmmm, maybe I will try being with a man. No! It's not like that. I was born like this. I knew from a very early age I was different. I found every boy in my class checking out girls and wanting to play video games. I wanted nothing more than to play with the girls and do their hair. I wanted to sing in chorus and dance on the dance team. I didn't want to throw a football or pick up a bat. I like getting my nails done and keeping a clean-shaven look. I'm super particular about my outfits and my stuff. I like soft skin and the smell of cologne. I like hairy chests and beautiful eyes. I tried falling to my knees to be the man my family wants me to be, but I can't. I cried myself to sleep for years. I begged God to take this away to heal me or fix me. I talked to my counselor at school, and she threatened to tell my mom. I told her I was joking and just wanted to see what she would say because I was curious about gay people. Her response was nothing shy of prejudice. She advised me not to look into evil things. She stated that it is best to steer clear of people like that. I went back to class thinking I needed to find a prom date. I had to make this believable. Thank God my best friend at that time was in the know and didn't care. She was the only friend I had who I confided in. She was the most amazing person. Unfortunately, due to her extravagant features, she was always being asked to go to the dances by her choice of boys. I was devasted, but as luck would have it, that year, she turned everyone down and went with me. No one could believe it. I couldn't even believe it. My mom was thrilled and swore this is how it all starts. "Oh, you and your high school sweetheart/best friend will be married soon." She was oblivious. I swear parents love denial more than anything else if it helps them sleep at night. In my head, I was thinking, lady, if only you knew she has all the wrong parts.

I wish Kay and I were closer because I feel like I could really use a friend, but the thing is, we have never been close. Kay is a rule follower, a good girl. I never understood why she and Nivea were best friends because Niv is the opposite. Niv doesn't care what people think or how they will react to her actions. She is Niv, and you get what you get. I wanted to tell Niv, but my fear is that since Kay is her best friend, my secret won't be safe. I know my mom will disown me, and my uncles will tell the whole family and probably beat me black and blue. I just want to go as far away from here as possible. I thought college was a great excuse. Since I am only nineteen, I have to get my mom to sign my federal aid. I have to use her income. I am moving to San Fran. It's the gay capital of the United States, and I need to be in the area where I and the love of my life are accepted. I am more in love with Keith than I ever thought possible. He's my best friend, and I never thought I would be happy living this lie. I was finally happy for the first time since realizing I was gay. I didn't care about lying or no one understanding my feelings and what struggles I had. I no longer wanted them too. I just wanted Keith. I clicked with him.

We met one day at the beach. I fell for him instantly. He is the most beautiful man I have ever seen. He's short and well built, but in a lean way. He's got all the definitions you dream of in a man. His eyes are green, and his Mexican skin is tan like toffee. He is fluent in Spanish, and when he talks to me in his native tongue, I lose my mind. He's smart and kind and has the most perfect smile. I love him more and more each day. We love to read poetry together and attend concerts and dance. We love to cuddle and drink expensive wine. The best times, though, are when we just hang at his apartment and listen to the ocean breeze blowing while lying naked in each other's arms. I've never felt so complete. How can something that feels so right be so wrong? How can so many people hate my life and my decisions? Why does it have any effect on them whatsoever? I can't imagine my life without Keith. He's my everything. I just need my mom to be present for five minutes and act like a mom. She's never been the same since my dad died. I swear, she makes it easier and easier to cut her off and move across the country to start a new life without her in it. I get it; he died, and we are all sad, but when you have kids to live for, and they are young and need you, isn't it your job to be there for them and put your own feelings aside? She is not a mother, but in fact, she is a figurative image that I rely on for nothing. She can rot in hell for all I care. Kay isn't on board with that. She still has hope in Mom. Well, Kay, you're on your own. We will never see eye to eye on that one. This is why me and my sister aren't close. She's way too perfect to be in my world. Always doing what is right and taking care of our mother's mistakes. She just won't fit, and Keith agrees, our life will be better without my family's involvement.

5

Nivea

It's one pm, and I am starving, but I know this new client is probably on her way. I cannot seem to kick the feeling that I know her. It is literally eating at me. My whole body is trying to remember... Levitt... Levitt... Miraaaanda... did she have a brother? Did I go to school with a Levitt? Just as I am thinking about food and Miranda, in she walks. Miranda is not what I expected. She is young and vibrant with super curly red hair like a real Irish would be. I cannot imagine this is her natural color because it is much too similar to Carrot Top, and that is the only known being on earth with hair like this. I stand up and walk towards her to greet her.

"Hi, you must be Miranda, I presume."

"Yes, in the flesh." And with this statement, I think, yea, you're not from here, but who are you? I walk Miranda to my chair and ask her what she is looking for today, and he explains to me she wants to get some color. To my surprise, this was her natural hair color. She explained to me she was looking for a few highlights to brighten up her face and wanted a cute haircut to match. I am stunned at this revelation. I am more than happy to accommodate her on this makeover as this is what I do. As I am doing her hair, I learn that I do, in fact, "know" Miranda. Not the way I thought, but I do know her. I remember a woman named Ashlee Levitt who lived on the end of Sunshine Rd., and she was elderly back then, so I assume this must be Miranda's grandmother. I decided to ask her what she was in town for and where she was from just to confirm my suspicions.

"So, Miranda, what brings you to Lutz? Are you on vacation?"

"No, not on vacation. As a matter of fact, I was born here, but we moved after a few years. You may know my grandmother, Ashlee Levitt. She has been a figure here for years."

BINGO! I knew she was related to this woman because why else would she be in town here in Lutz.

"Yes, of course, everyone knows your grandmother, although I have not seen her lately or for a long time for that matter."

"Well, I am in town because she passed. Unfortunately, my mom and I will be here for a while cleaning out her home and going through all her things."

"Oh my gosh, I am so sorry, Miranda! I really am! Please let me know if there is anything I can do."

"I appreciate that, but right now, I just want my hair to look good because I forgot how humid it was here. I am trying to be strong for my mom because I was not close to my grandmother. I never really saw her. It's like once we left Lutz, we never really came back."

"Well, let me be the first to say it is not the most endearing place. I think you may need a friend and a night out from all the work, though, so take my number and hit me up if you want to grab a drink sometime."

And with that, Miranda and I were now acquaintances. I don't trust new people, but I am a social butterfly, and if she likes to go out, then we will get along just fine.

6

Tiffany

My pager goes off constantly, and right now, I am on autopilot from working so many hours. I am currently working at Jackson Park in southside Chicago. I just completed med school, and my residency is another four to seven years to becoming an actual doctor. I love what I do with a passion. I love helping people. I always have. I wanted to be placed at Jackson Park. I knew the ER there would be filled with lots of cases that would teach me the ins and outs of surgery and complicated medical diagnosis. It is busy. It is never a dull moment. I work under Doctor Mychal. His name is spelled very uniquely, but it is pronounced just like Michael. He is from Pakistan. He is the most brilliant and amazing man I have ever encountered. He loves his job, and I swear the man never leaves the hospital. I want to be like that. I found out at a young age I couldn't have children. It's something that I learned over many therapy sessions with myself to let go of. I believe everything happens for a reason, and the reason I am not meant to have kids is that I am meant to help them. I see cases of extreme child abuse to gunshot wounds and gang green. It never ceases to amaze me what comes through that door. I graduated top of my class and was honored when I won an award for most successful medical president. I had a full scholarship when I started at my junior college, where I majored in pre-med. I attended Northwestern. It's a prestigious school and hard to get accepted, but I made it. My mother is beyond proud of me. She would never let anyone forget that her baby girl was going to be a doctor. She brought it up every chance she got.

~

I hear the intercom calling for Doctor Mychal, and I know that means me. I run to room 441, where I am met with him and several bystanders screaming, "Is he going to be okay? That's my baby. Save my baby. What are you doing? DOOOO SOMETHING!" This happens a lot when family is involved. I am in the hallway, pulling back the curtain, asking them all to move please so we can do our job. I try to be as polite as possible, but there is a life on the line, and the blood is on our hands. I follow the doc's orders, calling out vitals and what I see, which is several gunshot wounds to the chest and abdomen. I move faster than the speed of light, hooking him up to different machines and trying to talk to him. "Can you hear me? Hang on to my voice, stay with me. My name is Doctor Hamilton. Please try to stay calm and breathe in and out." I do my best to yell commands to the nurses who come to assist and stay attentive to the vitals airing on the machine. I focus on that sound which lets me know the heart is still in communication with us…beep…beeep…beeeep, and I stare at the lines going up and down, making peaks and valleys to assure me he is still alive. Quickly, I am dressing the wounds and holding pressure while screaming for nurse Linda to take my place. I rush to the sink and begin washing my hands for the total time of two minutes, making sure I am clean from fingertip to elbow. I assert myself gloved up in between the nurses and Dr. Mychal. I look at him, and he asks me, "What is next?" I take a long look at the victim. I know the time is ticking, and time is crucial, so I begin my analogy and say I need to operate, but first, I need X-rays to make sure I can safely remove the bullets. I begin delegating the tasks and calling up to the OR for a room. I need it prepped because I am about to perform surgery on a twenty-two-year-old man who was shot seven times in front of his mother!

When surgery is over, I can finally relax and tell the parents of the young man that he will be okay. He may never have full function again of his kidneys, but he will be able to walk, talk, and survive. The police are always involved in these situations, and before I get the chance to check on a patient, I normally have police asking if the patient is well enough for an interview. I make my rounds every day, and this patient will be in the ICU for a while. I am glad that I can tell his mother, "He is coming home; we just do not know when." I see these situations every day, and I think, maybe I am the lucky one that I will never carry an infant. I will never have a baby that I will have to worry about or a son who might be shot in the street. Those fears for me are far off and hard to imagine. My fears are so different from this mother. My fear begins with failing someone and losing a life because of my mistake. I have a lot on my plate, and the rush of adrenaline when in the ER is my drug of choice. I can't get enough even when I have a bad experience of losing a life. I want right back on the front line to deal with the next case. This is why they say I was born to be a doctor.

~

I pull up to my high rise, and I am so excited to take a hot bath and just relax. I live in downtown Chicago, and my views are indescribable. I love my condo. It is my safe haven, and I never feel stressed in here. I worked really hard to buy this condo and all of the stuff in it. I decorated it myself. I have really made a life for myself, and the only thing that is missing is someone to share it with. I've dated here and there and had the occasional fling, but I am incredibly busy trying to become a doctor, and time is not on my side. I would love to make time to date, but I am currently working upwards of ninety hours a week at the hospital. Sometimes, I don't get to come home; I literally shower there and nap in an empty room or on a lounge couch. My free time consists of catching up on sleep and having time to respond to my mom since she is the only one who texts me. I do have friends, but right now, our lives are just headed in different directions. Lots of people my age are looking for "the one," and I am looking for my career. As I walk up the long sidewalk in the lighted path, my shadow follows me. I feel like every step I take weighs a million pounds. I use my code to buzz myself in and head for the elevator. I push the button for the thirty-sixth floor and wait patiently for my stop. The hallway to my door is quiet like always, and I pull out my keys and unlock the door. I enter my condo and just breathe in the fresh scent of empty and lavender. I always have lavender scents about my place since it is supposed to soothe you and create a calm atmosphere. It is something I have needed to cope with my strenuous job and schooling for the last eight years. I literally kick my shoes off and begin undressing myself; home is so familiar. The beauty of the floor-to-ceiling glass windows surrounds me. I can see the Chicago skyline and the lights of the city. It is amazing to be up here, looking out naked and vulnerable, knowing no one can see me. I walk into my master bath, turning on my jacuzzi tub and filling it with hot water and bubbles from a basil-scented bath bomb. I light some candles and turn on some Motown. I grew up on Motown. It reminds me of my favorite past times. I slowly enter the water while singing to the Temptations when I hear my cell ringing. Of course, it would ring right now, and I know it is none other than my mother wanting to see how I am doing. She will have to wait; this bath is more important right now. I am in my Zen, and not even my mama can take that from me.

7

Kayla

I have decided that after last week's issues of my mom being her normal MIA, my brother deciding to leave for California, and Josh moving on with Jessica, I am due for a beach day. Today, I am packing a bag filled with fruit, chips, a book, and my headphones. I am not inviting Nivea because I swear that girl is always busy unless you catch her in advance. If she is not doing hair, she's out and about. She texted me that this weekend she would be hanging out with this girl Miranda who I guess is her new drinking buddy. I have never been much for drinking, and I know Niv secretly wishes I were her fish. She loves to kick back shots of just about anything as long as she is the center of attention and getting shitfaced.

My car is an old Honda, and I named her Sally a long time ago. She is my ride or die. I got her as my first car and paid for her all by myself from working at the diner. She is the only thing I have paid off or owned that is truly my own. I turn her on, and the song on the radio is none other than The All-American Rejects – *Gives You Hell.* How perfect for my cleansing of Josh. The only problem is, I am not a successful woman who made it without him. This song makes me realize how much I need to reach out to him. What's the harm anyways? Nivea hated Josh, which is why she probably thinks I need to ignore him, but I really just want to say hi. I miss him. I miss his voice, his texts, his gifts, his smile. I really miss him. I feel so lonely these days. One little text, that is all. I promise myself I will not make it a habit! I decide to wait till I stop driving and arrive at Howard Park Beach. That way, I can really focus on my text and what I want to say.

Jerimiah forged the papers for San Francisco State University because, of course, my mom was not available. I offered to help him pack and get ready for his big move, but he politely declined. He added that we are not that close and there is no reason to pretend like I am going to miss him. That's just it, though, I was going to miss him. I always thought that once I stepped up to take care of Jerimiah, he would be my best friend and love me like he did our mother, but somehow, I never seemed to take her place. It was almost as if he resented me trying to help raise him for her faults. I told him I wanted to fly with him to California and help him get set up and tour the school. He advised me he was leaving alone and was not a little kid anymore, so he didn't need his big sister tagging along. I am not sure why, but I feel as though Jerimiah is depressed. I think he feels neglected because he never had a mom or a dad who he grew up with in a loving household. I can't imagine he remembers my dad or anything related to having a father. Jerimiah has been so distant. School doesn't even start till August; it's only May, and he already packed and caught his flight. It was as if the only thing that stood between him and a future was this one signature. He left so abruptly it worried me. I haven't texted him or called him to see if he made it, and he hasn't offered any of that information either. Maybe he will meet a nice girl in SF, and I will have a sister-in-law to chat with. Maybe he will move back to Tampa and bring her here to live. I hope that one day, Jerimiah and I will find a way to break whatever barrier holds us back. I love my brother so much. He's all I have!

~

I pull up to the beach and park my car in front of a meter. I fill it with quarters and walk towards the sandy beach. I can smell the ocean and hear the waves crashing against the shore. It is a beautiful day, bright and sunny with a light breeze. I find my spot on the sandy beach and lay down a towel to sit on. I apply my sunscreen and search for my phone. Josh! Do I text him, or do I not text him? Ugh! I want to, but I know if I do, it could be bad. I decide to pull up our text thread. There it is in all its glory, the last text we ever sent to each other. I am a sucker, so deleting texts from him was never going to happen. Then the thought occurred to me, what if he had a new number? Omigosh, Kay, just send the text! I decide to be nice and send him a text that clearly shows I am still over him and happily moved on.

"Josh, hey, it's K! Just wanted to say I am so happy for you. I saw you found someone new. Hope you are well xo."

Phew! I can breathe now but feel sweaty. I am in panic mode. I decide I have to text someone else, but before I can, I get a reply. I am stunned! My phone shows one text unread from Josh! He responded. I am almost too afraid to open it and find out what it says. My hands are shaking, and I feel my mouth getting very dry. I decide I will read it and then not respond because I promised myself I would not do this, and I have to keep that promise. As I click to unlock my phone, my breathing gets shallow and heavy. I close my eyes and then open them, looking directly at the text.

"Who is Josh? Wrong number!"

Well, there's that. I feel myself returning to my normal state, but I am not sure if what I feel is relief or betrayal. Josh got a new number, and I have no clue what it is, and not only that, but I don't know what I expected from sending that text in the first place. I guess, in a way, I am glad he never saw it, and with that, I decide it is time to let go. I swipe right and hit the red delete button as fast as I can so I cannot change my mind. I can't help now but sit here and stare at my phone. That's it; just like that, he's gone. Gone like he never existed! You know what? I feel a lot better. I should've deleted those messages a long time ago. My day just got a whole lot better. I pop my earbuds in start the Apple Music playlist I made titled Relax K! And that is just what I do, soaking up the sun on the beach listening to sweet vibes of country music.

8

Nivea

Over the last couple of weeks, I have been super busy with my newfound part-time friend Miranda. I actually like this chick. She is a breath of fresh air in comparison to most people here. She is more eccentric and open-minded. I love her mom! I have spent most of my free time at her grandmother's, helping go through her things and clean out the house. It has been invigorating, to say the least. I actually like cleaning up this old lady's shit. I found some records that we played and danced to while taking shots of Patron. Believe it or not, this old lady had a liquor cabinet filled with alcohol like she was running a full-time bar. We have had our fun with liquor cabinet treasures, and with each shot comes more memories and tears and then laughs and sighs. I just sit and listen and soak up all the memorable experiences about Ashlee Levitt. I knew Mrs. Levitt but not well. I would see her in the grocery store or at the post office, you know, little run-ins here and there. I never really conversed with the woman or cared to for that matter. I know most people might feel weird being in a dead lady's home with her family they don't know, but I feel right at home here. I am actually hoping we find some real antiques or treasures we can sell. I find this daunting task to be helpful to my soul. It makes me feel good. Plus, I now have a friend in SC, and I can visit a new place. Miranda has already told me I am welcome anytime. I am excited to see what her beach town is like. Anywhere has to be better than Lutz. This washed-up town is boring as hell. Just a bunch of snobby white people who think they are better than everyone else. I hope Myrtle Beach isn't that kind of party because I am over attending these events!

"Mom, look what I found, it's Grandma's diary. Did you know she kept a diary?"

"No, I knew she liked to journal, and she was an English teacher, but I never knew she kept one in her later age."

"Maybe there will be some interesting stuff in here. Mom, seriously, let's read this tonight!"

"I don't know, Randa, it may be private, and it's her diary, not ours. Let me put it up for now, and I will decide later what we should do with it."

I was surprised Miranda's mom cared. I mean, after all,

the lady is dead. She's not coming back looking for her diary. She isn't going to get mad and haunt us for reading it. I wanted to chime in, but my opinion isn't always welcomed or warm. Not that I normally care, but for the sake of not offending my new friend and her mother, who are burying their dead loved one, I will keep my mouth shut. However, I make no promises once we really start drinking. Besides, I am curious, what does an old woman journal about? It's not like anything happened in her day. The book is probably downright boring at best, but I'd still like to read it! Maybe I can talk Miranda into sneaking it out without her mom knowing. I'll think of something.

9

Kayla

I heard a scream and then someone yelling outside in the backyard. I got up from the couch where I was sitting and headed to the window. No surprise there; it's my mother fighting with my uncle Rodney. I take a deep breath and prepare myself for the negotiating tactics I will have to use to get her to calm down and come inside. I walk out to the familiar backyard that leads up to my driveway. The house I grew up in is no longer cared for like when I was a child. This house has no flower beds or gardens, no ponds or fresh-cut grass. Everything is overgrown and falling apart. Our house is the best lot because we have the whole corner. People always covet the corner lot. It has the biggest yard and the best view. Tin Smith Circle is a quaint street, and most people know your name or your relative's names. There are no crimes committed, other than my father's, of course, and it's safe. My uncle Rodney is the sheriff and has been my whole life. He is a good man. Rodney is special to me because after my father died, he stepped up to be there for me while I cared for my brother and dealt with my father's death. He's still there for me with my mother's indiscretions. I am thankful for Rodney, but he would never replace my father. Rodney is set in his ways and strict as they come. He is not going to let you slide on a ticket you deserve. It's just not the type of cop he is, and everyone knows it. He goes over things with a fine-tooth comb, and he has a reputation for being a bit of a prick to his squad. He is the no-nonsense no-tolerance type of guy. Rodney is big and has one of those guts that hangs over his pants. You know a cop who loves the donuts a bit too much. He enjoys a good meal, no doubt. He loves his wife and kids, and I'd say he is a good father figure and husband, but he's not my dad. Rodney and my mom are close in age, and he feels responsible for her. I guess it's similar to how I feel responsible for Jerimiah. Rodney is the one brother who will never give up on my mom. They have a special bond, and it shows. This is just another routine night for Rodney and Slim.

∼

"Hey, Uncle Rodney."

"Hey, Kay, you want to help me with your momma?"

"Of course." My mother begins to scream how she doesn't need any help and to get my hands off of her. She is combative and smells of old beer and nasty stale cigarettes. She is screaming so loud I am afraid the neighbors are going to file another complaint against her. It's only six pm, and already I have to put my mother to bed. The scene is all but embarrassing, and I am itching to get her in the house. My mom is tiny, and since Rodney is such a big man, I beg him each time to just carry her inside, but he's always respectful of his dear old Slim. I am frustrated, but this time, no tears. They haven't come in eons because I am numb to nights like these. They don't even phase me anymore. I no longer get upset; I just follow suit, and we do the same thing we always do, try to reason with an unreasonable woman.

Finally, I get my mom inside and lay her on the couch. I offer her some leftovers from the diner, and she declines like always.

"Mom, you have to eat. Trust me, it will help you feel better, especially with soaking up some of the alcohol."

"Don't tell me what to do, Kayla. You're not the boss of me. I don't want any food; I want you to leave me alone."

At this point, I know I am not going to get anywhere, so I warm up the food and place two aspirin, a blanket, the roast beef, and a big cup of water next to her. By morning, it will be gone. I can only hope that one day she gets the help she needs before it's too late.

In my room, I can hear her talking, but I know no one is there. I can tell she is still agitated. Sometimes I wonder what my dad would do if he saw her like this and how he would handle this situation. I am exhausted from working and then caring for her. It's like having a toddler. The next noise I hear is her throwing up, and I drop my head in disbelief. No, Mom, no, please, no, not tonight! Ugh! I get up and grab the bleach and bucket along with a sponge, the same orange sponge I've used a thousand times to clean up her puke.

"Mom, here, let me help you to the shower."

"Kayla, I am sorry. Kay, are you mad at me? You don't love me, do you?"

This is the same broken record. Once she begins to sober up, she becomes the victim who no one loves, and she needs validation that she is still the loving mother she used to be. I play along, not because I agree or want to, but for the sake of upsetting her with the truth. She cries in the shower while I scrub the tile floor and wipe down the coffee table. I get to the bathroom and help her wash her hair and then brush it out. After helping her get dressed and into her bed, I head to my room. It's eleven pm now, and I have to be at work at five am for the opening shift. I lie in my bed, and tears fill up in my eyes. It's at this point I decide to text Jerimiah. I really miss him!

"J, wherever you are, I hope you know I love you. Another fun night with Mom. I miss you, J."

I roll over and close my eyes. It's been a long day, and to-morrow will be here before I know it. I whisper, *"Goodnight, J. Goodnight, Dad."*

10

Kayla

I decided to go to Nivea's shop today and get myself a mini makeover. I mean, I am not a girl who wears a lot of make-up or dresses up very often, but in my defense, I am simple. I just like it better that way. I like my bun I wear almost every day since working at the diner includes that in the dress code, and it has just become apart of who I am. Besides, when you live in the Florida heat, you have no choice but to be natural. Well, I see it that way, but Niv, she is always done up to the nine. I have never been one of those girls, and I never will be. I am thinking today that I want to do something fun, though, just not too crazy. My hair is long and super straight, but it's never had any color, so it's just a mousy brown. I think I'd like to add some purple streaks, which is going to make for a very happy Nivea! She has been dying to get her hands on my head since she began this journey of becoming a stylist. I cannot count how many times in high school she begged for me to be her guinea pig. I always declined, of course, but she never could understand how her best friend wouldn't support her. I told her she could practice doing my brows and giving me a trim, but I am not fancy like that. Eventually, she came to terms with it and let it go. Today, though, I am feeling brand new, like a woman who needs a change. I might even add some layers to my hair, something else I have never done before. Once I cleanse my hair of its natural beauty to add this violet vibrant new look, I am going to lunch with Nivea, and I cannot wait. I am in desperate need of some girl time and a glass of wine.

I walk into Nivea's salon, and I can hear her on the phone with a client towards the back, so I take a seat in one of the stylist's chairs. It used to bother me she didn't have a waiting room, but now I understand why. She is the only one who works here, and she jumps from client to client, overbooking herself all day. This is how she does it. She uses these four round mint green chairs to work on clients separately and together. It works for her. I haven't been in here for a long time, and it looks different than I remember. I guess I never paid it much attention before. Niv has always had a career and been a go-getter, and I have just been a waitress. I never felt jealous, but now, sitting here seeing what she's done, it's like seeing it for the first time. I can't explain it, but now I feel a twinge of jealousy. She's teeming with success, and I am over here serving hot plates. Why haven't I chosen to do something with my life? What am I so afraid of?

"Hey, Lady."

"Oh, hey, Niv." I stand to give her a hug, and she kisses me on the cheek and grabs my shoulders to push me away while she stares at my face. I am feeling awkward, but I am guessing she is designing me in her head, much like any artist does with their blank canvas.

"I am so excited for this and have waited so long! I am going to make you the prettiest girl in all of Lutz! Not that you aren't already, but Kay Kay, you know I got you! Just wait!"

Those words sent me into fear, and not because I doubt her skills, but because I am not one for change, and her tone makes me realize she might just go overboard because this is her one chance!

"Niv, nothing crazy, please. I am only looking for a couple pieces of color, and I don't want to walk out of here looking crazy. I do have to work tomorrow."

Niv looked at me like I had eight heads but assured me she knew me and how afraid I was, so I needed to trust her. Trust wasn't my strong suit, so I was taking leaps and bounds right now by even sitting in this chair. I just decided to relax and told myself, "*Hey, what's the worst that can happen?*"

When my hair was finished, Niv spun me around in the chair to see my new self for the first time, and I stared at the person in the mirror for a long while. I couldn't speak because, for the first time in my life, I finally recognized myself. I finally saw the person I have been hiding behind all this time. I saw a beautiful girl with gorgeous waves that glowed with purple strands weaved in them. I saw a girl who looked innocent but hurt. I saw a girl who was coming out of her shell and finding her way. A girl who was changing for the better and making waves that no one could stop.

"I love it, Niv, I really love it, you did such a good job, and I don't know why I was so afraid because I should've let you do this years ago! Omigosh, I really feel like a brand-new person, I can't even explain it."

"See, I told you. I know what I am doing, and I wouldn't let you down."

"No, you never do, but now I am starving and ready to show off my hair. Let's go."

We headed into town, which isn't much of a place to begin with, but again, Lutz is a small suburb of Tampa. However, we do have the Market Hall, which features Tampa's Premium Outlets, and it's about as nice as it gets in our part of town. We head straight for Longhorn Steak House and start out with a glass of champagne to celebrate my new look. I am excited to be out with Niv. I really miss how much we used to hang out, and right now, being with her has made me realize I am lost without her. She really is my best friend, and no one can take her place.

We sat there laughing and talking for hours. I told Niv how my mom had another drunken night episode where she made one of her epic debuts in the yard with Uncle Rodney, and of course, Niv was supportive and told me she was sorry. She told me about her new friend Miranda and how much she really enjoys her company and helping clean out Mrs. Levitt's house. She told me they found a diary, and she is interested in what an old lady would write down. We talked about her salon and how busy she was and what dating apps she was using. We laughed and drank till the sun went down. I miss Nivea, and I miss nights like this. We took a selfie together and posted it to Facebook with the caption Best Friends Forever!

$\sim$

When I got home, I was in the best mood. I couldn't wait to take a shower and just relax in my bed. However, the world had different plans for me. I thought nothing could ruin my night, but on my way home, I got a call from Uncle Dave, and he said my mom was rushed to Tampa Medical and I needed to meet them there. Here we go again, another night of taking care of Mom. I wonder what it's like to be a normal family and have your mom worry about you. I turned around at the next intersection and hopped on the highway to the city. I sped as fast as I could without drawing attention to myself because the last thing I needed was a ticket. I pulled into the hospital parking lot and headed for the emergency room doors. Once inside, I was greeted by Uncle Dave, his wife Anna, and my other uncle, Ben. Dave gave me a big hug and said, "Long time no see. You look good, Kay. I love the streaks of purple, when did that happen?" Well, I wanted to say, *not long enough ago for me to enjoy it before your sister ruins another night,* but instead, I opted for a simple, "Today, actually, how's my mom?" Before he could answer, my aunt Anna spoke up and said, "You know, Kay, it's not fair you have to deal with this, and I really think it's time you move out of your mom's house. You shouldn't be babysitting her; she is a grown woman, and no child should have to do what you do." I agreed, but the thing is, my aunt Anna has never liked my mom. They never did get along. Uncle Dave and my mom are the closest in age. The birth order is Rodney, Ben, my mom—Joanna, and then Dave. Aunt Anna has only known my mom as a drunk, never as a mom or anything else for that matter. Uncle Dave sides with his wife a lot because, well, that's what husbands do, but Uncle Ben is not married, he's divorced and had no kids, so he doesn't say much in regard to parenting. I smiled at Aunt Anna and then told her I appreciate her concern; however, I know my mom needs me. She didn't like my answer and signed an exaggerated breath and then rolled her eyes and looks at my uncle Dave and asks how much longer till they can leave. I didn't say much; I just took my seat and waited for the explanation. Uncle Dave ignored his wife and told me that my mom had alcohol poisoning and that this time it was bad. He went on to explain that her liver was shutting down from her drinking and that the doctors were removing one of her kidneys. I wasn't sure how to take the news. I was concerned for my mom but also for Jerimiah, who hasn't so much as texted or called me. "Has anyone notified J about my moms' condition?" No one did. No one so much as even shot him a quick text. Uncle Ben finally spoke only to say, "Isn't he off at school somewhere out west? He's probably busy and doesn't need to be bothered." Then it occurred to me, why am I the one who is bothered? Why is he off Scott free while I give up my nights in my twenties to clean up puke for a grown woman? We sat in silence for what felt like hours, and finally, the doctor came out to say she was going to be just fine, but she was not going home for a while. Is it rude that this made me happy? I was glad, and I pretty sure didn't hide the expression well enough on my face. I didn't care, though. I just asked if we could see her so I could say goodnight and go home! I just can't keep doing this anymore. I think maybe for once I agree with my aunt Anna; it's time for my mom to take care of herself!

11

Tiffany

This morning around four am, we had a family come into the ER stating that the father was unresponsive. The wife and daughters were a mess crying and screaming that they needed a doctor. Doctor Mychal was in surgery already, so I was on deck. I came in asking the first responders what was going on? While I was trying to get information to potentially save this man's life, the wife began screaming, "I don't want that nigger touching my husband. Keep your paws off of him. Get me someone else! Get me a real doctor! This black bitch is going to kill him!" It's amazing she knew I was an African American, but on the same token, she missed the part where I share her color and heritage as well. She was blinded by the tan I have and the poofy hair I wear on my head. She missed my educated brain that gives me the skills to save her husband. My 4.4 GPA and my honors achievements. She didn't see the ribbons I wore at graduation for being in the top three percent of my graduating class or the first picked draft to work for Doctor Mychal. Nope, she could only see my color. Of course, I can get her an all-white doctor, but will they have my skills? My knowledge? My abilities? Probably not! It's a busy night in here. However, I have to mind my manners and take the hate with a grain of salt. It kills me to apologize for the color of my skin. It hurts my heart to have to pretend I am not black, but if it means saving a human's life, then I will do just that.

Growing up here in one of Chicago's most prestigious neighborhoods, I was exposed to lots of parties and affluent people. I grew up in Lincoln Park, and my mother was a successful broker, and my father was a professor. I attended the best schools and took part in gymnastics and piano lessons. Eventually, my talents advanced, and I was in a club and competed at the state level as a gymnast. My father taught theology, so I was prone to being a history buff. My parents chose not to have any other children as I was their pride and joy. My mother raised me to be a kind, bright, remarkable young lady because she told me the world would not accept me. I am mixed, and as a biracial woman, I have to decide on a daily basis which race I most relate to because people have a hard time accepting you as both. I get hell from both sides. For instance, at work, the black woman will make snood remarks about my light skin and tell me I am not a true Sista! I just brush it off, but deep down, I feel like an outcast. At school, growing up, I was treated like the white girl. I am neither, just white or black, but I feel like everyone expects me to choose a side and stick to it. I remember attending a piano recital and hearing a little girl whisper to her mom that my hair was frizzy and my mom should learn how to brush it. I remember my first day at summer camp for gymnasts and being pointed at by the white girls who said my braids made me look like a man, and by the end of summer, I was called everything from brownie to nigger. I have never felt comfortable in my own skin, and I have suffered for a long time trying to understand the hate people have towards me as a biracial individual. When I first began med school, I remember feeling exposed and like I had to prove myself. It's a feeling none of my white friends understood. Living in an affluent area, most of my friends were white, but I never really knew if they were my real friends. It's hard to say if I was just a ploy for them to look like they weren't racist or if they really did like me. I spent many nights crying to my mom, telling her I felt lost and unaccepted, and she would tell me that was a part of life as a black woman. She explained to me that even if you had the smallest drop of black in your blood line, 1/8th to be exact, you were considered black. She told me I had a fighting chance to prove that black women can be doctors and a good one at that. She pushed me hard. My mom pushed me to be the best gymnast, the best pianist, and the best student. She stressed the importance to me of being seen as the underdog. I always felt like my mom referred to me as black because she was black. It was weird how I never felt like she truly saw me as biracial. I find it hard to date and find someone who will accept me for being a combination of races. I hear some of my colleagues say, "Well, in the winter, you have white passing girl." I am not looking to pass as white or gain the so-called white privilege. I just want to be me and not have to choose. People don't realize how hard it is to find where you fit in when you aren't wanted by either side. I experienced a lot of racism when I was younger with my braided hair and dark brown skin. As I have gotten older, my tan is not so prominent, as I never lie or play in the sun. I honestly don't have time. My hair is still a curly afro, but I get Keratin straighteners to keep it at bay. My features are all big. I have big pouty lips that most white girls pay big money for, my eyes are huge, and I have super long lashes. I am tall and stand at 5'8 without heels. I have a tan compared to the white girls but nothing crazy. My nose is average and pierced twice! I have two rings on my left nostril. I am closing in on 150 pounds, but it's all in the back and thighs. My waist has always stayed small, but my lower half is a bit thicker. I have very cut arms, and I owe that to gymnastics and genetics. My chest is an average C cup, and therefore, I see myself as your everyday average woman. When people meet me, they always seem to feel the need to ask me where I am from. Well, actually, I am from here, Chicago. It blows my mind. They act as if I am some kind of exotic being from outer space. Honestly, I don't see what difference it makes how I look. As long as I do my job to save your life or your family members' life, it should have no bearing on what I look like. My mother did make me learn a second language, and for that, I am forever grateful because when I let my Spanish tongue take over, it really gets the attention of bystanders. Either way, I love the way I look; I just need to figure out how to get everyone else to accept it. How to teach the world not to be blinded by color. I wish for one day everyone was color blind. I wish they could no longer see you as a race or ethnicity, but we were all orange. No one had special features, and we just looked the same! Could you imagine what a boring world that would be? I think it would be the wake-up call we have all been waiting for, though! A world where we all wear the same color and look exactly alike, a world without diversity, a world where we weren't blinded by color!

12

Jerimiah

I am loving California! San Francisco is everything I have dreamed of and more. Keith and I landed an apartment in the bay area, and we walk everywhere. We have yet to need a car with the BART system in place here. Life is beautiful. We've visited Alcatraz and Treasure Island; we hang out at Pier 39 and go for hikes. The beaches are beautiful, and the people are incredible here. No one judges us for being a rainbow couple. We can hold hands in public and hang out at gay bars. It's the most amazing experience ever.

I landed a job working for Twitter as a customer service agent, and Keith took a job as a lifeguard. Together, we make decent money, and the best part is we spend every weekend at the beach, and I sit right by his lifeguard stand and spend his whole shift with him. We have already met several other gay couples who have invited us out, and we are considering a housewarming party for our new place. This has been a journey, and my twentieth birthday is coming up, and I want to celebrate in a big way. Keith is older than me, and he takes great care of me, so I am sure he has something extravagant planned. I can't wait to find out what it is.

I haven't even checked in at home because I already know how the conversation will go. Kay will blab on about her boring life of working at the diner and tell me about how Mom has gotten worse since I left, and I should call her blah blah. I actually feel free and like myself for the first time ever in my life. I never had a coming-out party in Lutz, and if I tried, it would have been shut down by my uncles. They seem to rule not only the town but everyone in it. That place was going to be the death of me. I was living a lie and hiding behind a façade of mixed emotions. I felt trapped and suffocated, and every day, I wanted to kill myself. If I hadn't met Keith when I did, I might not be here today. I don't expect everyone to understand my struggles or my fears. I know a lot of close-minded people think I can just turn this off like a faucet. Wake up tomorrow and not be gay, marry a woman, and have babies. Live a life that is pleasing to God and others. I tried, though, and I was miserable. I felt like I couldn't bear the person I was becoming because it was for someone else's pleasure. I had to live for myself, and although I am young, I know this is what I wanted. This is what feels right.

I saw a text from my sister a couple of weeks ago, and I ignored it. She was super sweet like always, but that's just who

Kay is. She always tries to do what's right and walk the straight and narrow. I don't know exactly when we became strangers, but I would like to think it was mutual. I feel like growing up, Kay resented the fact that Mom got worse. She decided it was unfair for her to have to raise me. I felt like a burden to her. She constantly seemed depressed and stressed out. She never had the loving, fun spirit my mom did. Not that I should have expected it since she wasn't my mom, she was my sister. The thing is, Kay changed after Dad died, and she never seemed to regain herself again. The bright light that shone around her wasn't dim; it was nonexistent. She was introverted and quiet. She stopped doing things that most kids loved. She started taking care of household duties, and by the time she was fifteen and I was eleven, she was so robotic it was as if there was nothing there but an autopilot button she used to start her day. She did the cleaning the cooking, helped with my homework, and picked up my mom from her many stumbles. She made my lunch and washed my clothes. She didn't ask how my day went or if I wanted to have a friend over; she just kept it neutral like I was her checklist.

Pack J's lunch.

Wash J's Clothes/bedding.

Make dinner.

Tell Jay to shower.

Check J's homework.

Tell him to go to bed.

Once I was checked off, she ventured to her room, and I didn't see her again till I was her morning routine. Life became very lonely. My mom was on a rocky road to AA, and my sister was trying to do everything to hold the family together while never really mourning our father, and then here I am just trying to find anyone I can confide in about my sexuality. I was never going to talk to Kay because I could tell she didn't want to be my mom. Taking on all this responsibility was far too much for her, so adding my homosexual issues was going to push her over the edge.

I learned to deal with things on my own. Keep them bottled up inside of me. I learned to let go of the image I held onto for years of the perfect mother I had. By the time I was a teenager, she had been to rehab nine times and failed all nine. I never did the normal high school thing like playing sports or going to school dances because how was that possible? I had no involvement from my mother. I could not take myself to get clothes for a dance, and even though my uncle Rodney stepped up to help out and be our father figure, I was afraid of him. He never gave me the friendliest of vibes. I found him to be tough as nails and harder on me for being a boy. He never seemed to take to me like he did Kay. I swear if I weren't a boy, he would have loved my dad being gone and him having two daughters to dote on. The thing is, in a way, I was a daughter too; I just couldn't show him that. He never would have accepted it.

13

Kayla

My brother has been gone for over a month now, and I am left to deal with all my mother's shortcomings on my own. Not that we ever vibed and chatted it up, but at least I knew someone who understood my struggles. I got a call this morning that it was time for my mother to be released, and therefore, I took the day off work to prepare myself. I am not looking forward to bringing her home, although I hope she is sober enough to have a tough conversation. I mean, if she wasn't sober, I would wonder how she got drunk in her hospital bed, although I would not be surprised knowing my mother; she probably drank the disinfectant and whatever else she could find in that room that had any form of alcohol in it. For my sake, I am going to pretend she still has some decency and decided against alcohol while healing from an alcoholic coma.

During the last two weeks, I have spent a lot of time by myself. This new me was really thriving. I actually went looking for apartments because even though I feel responsible for my mother and her failed attempts at parenting, I am done being her babysitter. If J can leave and go live his life, then why can't I? Growing up, I spent a lot of time with my uncle Rodney, who was like a father to me. Rodney was the one who took care of me and J each time my mother was sent off to rehab. Uncle Rodney was the one who drove me to my prom and paid for my hair appointment at the salon. He was the one who dropped off casseroles his wife made and taught me how to cook them in the oven. Uncle Rodney tried, he really did, but at the end of the day, he wasn't my father. I loved him, but I wish for once he would stop enabling my mom. Maybe if I go, he won't hold me to the standard of helping him take care of his sister, who clearly doesn't want our help. My mother is slowly killing herself, and I have a front-row seat to her deteriorating. I wonder why Uncle Rodney doesn't just say she is horrible. It's like he constantly feels responsible for her actions. I get it, you're her big brother, but honestly, at some point, you have to give her tough love and stop hand-holding. I appreciate my uncles, but I also resent them. At times, I feel like they just expect me to be there and take care of her forever. Give up my whole life, as if I didn't already give up my childhood.

The first thing my momma and I will be discussing is my new address. I took the liberty of scoping out several apartment complexes while I had no one to care for but me. I loved taking these tours of models that showed me what I was getting should I chose this floor plan. I found an apartment by Market Hall, walking distance, in fact, right on Cypress. I thought for a second about asking Nivea if I could move in with her. I would still be close to home since she is only two streets over from me and has a whole house to herself. Nivea inherited her parents' home when they moved out west to Arizona for retirement. Nothing about the humidity in Florida was aesthetically pleasing to them. They chose Arizona for its dry climate and beautiful views. They didn't owe much left on their home, so they initiated a rent to own with their only daughter. Niv jumped on the opportunity to turn her childhood home into her own. I just can't see Niv and me living in her house together and calling it ours. I want something I can call my own. This apartment was perfect. It was a studio that overlooked the pool. Upon walking in, you are greeted by cool tiles that accent perfectly with the light blue walls. The beige tiles cover the entire living room and kitchen, including the small bathroom. I would literally only need a pull-out couch or a futon to place in the living room, and that would suffice as my bedroom. The living room was to the left and fairly small, so one couch, a TV, and a coffee table would be pushing it. The kitchen featured a small bar, and I could put at least two chairs there for eating. The place seemed so bright, with a beautiful balcony off the living room with a pool view. I had access to laundry, a gym, and a pool. Not much more I could ask for. I got my own parking space under a covered panel, and that was all I needed. It felt right. It felt like it was time. Time to move on, time to grow up, and time to leave the nest. It was the part about telling my mom I dreaded. The fear that if she were not sober, it wouldn't go very well, and if she were sober, it still wouldn't go well. The thing is, sober Slim makes for a loving, overly sweet emotional person, and drunk Slim makes for a rude, loud, abusive version. There is no in-between. No happy medium. Today, I am prepared for sober emotional Slim because a part of me is hoping she didn't drink the cleaning supplies.

I pulled up to the hospital in Sally, my reliable Honda, and parked as close to the entrance as I could. Since I am a little early, I decide to take a little detour inside the hospital to Starbucks. I love Starbucks, and I am forever grateful the hospital has one. I approach the counter and lift my sunglasses to my head as the barista walks over to greet me. "Well, hey there, how are ya? What can I make for you today? By the way, I love your romper; it's (finger snap) fire." Now I know firsthand this guy with his twang in his voice and his tight jeans and rainbow pin on his apron must be fruity. I wasn't raised to accept gay people, but today, I am too occupied with my own life to let this creature of a man in front of me get me angry. "I'd like a grande vanilla latte, kids temp, with a chocolate chip cookie, please." He is overly happy and excited to make my drink and get my cookie, and as he tries to strike up a small talk convo, I let him know I am in a rush because I am not a mean girl, but I have zero tolerance for this type of behavior. There is no excuse for a man to act like a woman or to talk using words like fierce and fire to explain my outfit. I get tired of the rainbows, and I truly don't understand why he is the face of Starbucks in a major hospital. That's Tampa for you; the city lets anyone in. Tobin, as his name tag states, put my drink and cookie on the pickup counter, and I grabbed it quickly and disappeared to a seating area to enjoy it in peace. While I sat there staring out the window, I noticed an alert from Facebook Messenger. It was from Josh! Josh? Wait, Josh sent me a message. I almost couldn't get my fingers to work to unlock my iPhone. I sat for a minute, taking a few deep breaths and sipping my latte to calm myself. How am I going to open this message right now, and what will it say? I wasn't sure if I should open it right now or wait, so I decided to wait. I locked my phone and finished my latte and cookie. I headed for the elevator and pushed the number four to pick up my mother.

~

Getting my mom in the car was a disaster. She was confused and delirious. I kept asking the nurse what was wrong with her, and she advised me my mom was on pain meds from having surgery. Great! Another addiction to add to her list. Once we got to the house, I helped her out of the car and onto the porch, where we sat down. I looked at her in disbelief that this was my mother! Joanna Romano, what happened to you? She is nothing but a shell. A withered woman who looks fifteen years her elder. She has the stringiest blonde hair I have ever seen, and I can't believe I have never noticed this before. She is so thin her cheeks are sunken in and her eyes droop. Her eyes are yellow and bloodshot. Her skin wrinkled and stuck to her body from what I imagine is a case of severe dehydration. How have I never noticed before? She looks awful. Nothing like the beautiful woman I remember. Full of life and happy and clean with a face full of makeup and natural beauty. She looks ill now. I actually thought I might be making a mistake. How can I leave her like this? What kind of daughter leaves their mom like this? She needs me. She clearly needs me, and now I am having regrets that I signed that lease on impulse. I never do things like that, but this new hairdo and attitude were fitting me so perfectly I thought it must be right. Now I am sitting here staring at this woman and thinking, "You're a mess, and I am a selfish daughter trying to leave you like this. How could I have been so stupid?" I get up and move to sit next to her. I grabbed her fragile hand and put it in mine. "Mom, I want you to get better. I think you should go back to rehab and get some real help; I'm worried about you." Just like that, as if the wind blew and she was someone else, she stood up and told me to mind my business. She walked into the house and slammed the porch door. The next thing I heard was cabinets slamming open and shut, and I knew. I knew she was looking for any ounce of alcohol, but I already cleared the house of any temptation while she was in the hospital. I take a deep breath because I already know tonight will be a long one. Pain pills and alcohol are not a good combination. I decided to text Mr. H., "*Sorry, Mr. H, I am going to need to take tomorrow off too. I will be in touch. Right now, I got to tend to my mother.*"

14

Nivea

Today, I am running late for Mrs. Robins, and I assume she will be understanding, but I am certain she will also be on time. I am doing my best to get to the shop, but of course, as Florida does in all its glory, we have severe rain and thunderstorms. I never seem to function quite as well when it rains. I am always more tired and can't seem to get up. Today is extra bad being that I started my period last night; it just adds gasoline to the fire. On my way to work, I decided to stop and get a Red Bull from the gas station. At this point, I just need a pick-me-up.

I pull into my usual parking spot and grab my umbrella to keep from looking like a wet mop all day! As I am running across the parking lot, I spot Mrs. Robins's car and head towards it to help her out. To my surprise, she is on the passenger side. I approach the car, and she opens the door, and OH MY GOD, it's her! I couldn't believe it! I stood in shock for what must have been longer than I realized because Mrs. Robins asked me if I was okay. "Oh, yes, I'm sorry, I didn't realize you had someone bringing you in today." She smiled and looked over at her driver, "Yes, let me introduce you to my granddaughter Jessica. She is from Miami, and now she lives up here with me. I was hoping you could do her hair too." I was stunned. How could this trashy thing be related to Mrs. Robins! Not my Mrs. Robins! Not Jessica The Realist who was dating Josh the asshole! The one who dated my best friend and broke her heart! No, this was not happening! How could this be happening? "Of course, Mrs. Robins, I would love to do your granddaughter's hair. Hi, Jessica. I'm Nivea, so nice to meet you." In my head, those words sounded much different. They went more like, "You whore I am going to shave your head and throat punch you till you can't stand up!" I am glad now they didn't come out like that because that would have been bad, and I do have a reputation for not holding my tongue. I'm sure my face gave it all away, but I decided to play it cool because today I was going to play investigator! I was going to get all the 411 I could and pretend I was clueless as to who Josh was and who she was. I mean, I did always want to be an actress, so this was my chance at my first academy award.

"Hi, Nivea, it's nice to meet you too," Jessica replied.

Inside the shop, I am shaking a little, and I blame it on my nerves and the added caffeine from my Red Bull, but I am eager to get started. I begin first with Mrs. Robins and move as fast as I can without making it obvious that I am ready to throw her under the hood dryer where she can't hear a word I am saying to her precious Jessica!

"Okay, Jessica, I am ready for you. Please come over and have a seat. Tell me what you are thinking you want to get done."

"I was hoping to get my hair like this picture on my phone. It's not a recent picture, but it's a photo of what I used to look like, and I loved my hair back then." When I took the phone from her, I couldn't believe this was the same person. Being me, I am so quick to speak without thinking, but the astonishment was all over my face. When I finally looked up at her to compare the photos, she was staring at me with the most terrified face! I was a bit taken aback. It was almost as if she was embarrassed this was her. I would've been proud this was me! She looked amazing in this picture. She was posing in a white dress at a bar, I presume in Miami. Her dress was short and sparkly, and she had these red heels on that looked expensive, and I wondered how she could afford them. Her face was flawless with gorgeous makeup, and her smile was beautiful. It was almost overly good to be true. Her hair was a gorgeous platinum blonde and had a few low lights of caramel. I thought to myself, "Well, Niv, we can do makeovers, but we can't perform miracles." But I am glad that part didn't reach my tongue and stayed in my head. I looked at Jessica and handed her phone back.

"You know what? I can get you really close to this look, but maybe not exactly this look in one appointment. If I am being honest, it will be a long process, and I am willing to do it if you have the time." This is my job, my livelyhood, so for as much as I might want to ruin her hair right now to make her ugly so Josh won't like her anymore, I can't. I have to make this money and keep my reputation. This is about business, not Kayla and her affairs. Besides, she just decided she is moving on in life and has become a new person. I am sure she is going to be just fine with me making her ex-boyfriend's new chick a stunning eight out of ten.

Once I've mixed up the bleach and color and applied it to her hair, it was time to brush out Mrs. Robins, who had decided to nap while under the hood dryer. Mrs. Robins was up front sitting by Jessica. I knew I had lost my opportunity to gain any details, but I was okay with that since I wanted to get paid and not lose a client. I didn't harass Jessica during her color process because she was very timid and quiet. I felt like I was working on a doll no one wanted because it wasn't pretty anymore. I sat down to join the two of them and began talking with Mrs. Robins.

"So, any plans for you and Jessica for this summer? You must love having the company."

"You know what, sweetheart? Jessica moved up because she was badly mistreated by my son. She had a great life and was raised by her single mother, who did an excellent job taking care of her. Unfortunately, my son, who never did get himself together, was released from prison only to fight for his daughter. The courts in Miami agreed she needed to have her father in her life. Baby, you know what? He may be my son, but he was abusive as hell. He beat Jessica and stopped taking care of her like her mother did. He was nothing shy of horrific. The things this poor child went through are unforgivable and inconceivable. Listen here, sweet pea, I flew to Florida and took her from him. There was no way I was going to let this go on, and had I known sooner, I would have saved her from his wrath. I can't change what happened, but I am going to do my darndest to help her cope now with life. She is doing better each day. Isn't that right, Jess? Mee-maw is super proud of you." I was sitting there, not able to speak. Here, Kayla and I were judging this girl and calling her trash when in reality, she wasn't. She had a mother who loved her and took excellent care of her. She was in an affluent area and looked like she came from money in her picture. It broke my heart to think her whole world was turned upside down because, yet again, the courts didn't think a failing father should be kept from his daughter. He took her light and her soul piece by piece. She had a fear about her that spoke volumes about what she must have been through. Her quiet, shy demeanor and how she stayed looking at the floor and felt self-conscious about any and everything you mentioned pertaining to her looks. I actually felt like shit. I really needed to stop judging people based on appearances. I should have given her and Josh the benefit of the doubt! Oh my gosh, Josh! He's such a jerk! He's going to ruin this girl. Break what little is left of her! How do I bring this up? How do I tell her he is not a good guy without telling her he is not a good guy? I have to say something. I have to. I am just going to come out with it. No beating around the bush!

"Jessica, I am friends with Josh on Facebook, and I saw he posted a pic of you recently stating that the two of you are dating. How did you meet? I've known Josh forever, and he's not the best guy. I just want you to be careful."

"I met Josh at a conference for abused victims. I guess he never talked about his issues with anyone before. No one from his hometown even knew he was so angry inside from what he was experiencing. When we met, it was like I finally had someone who understood my pain, and he felt the same way. He's my best friend and everything I need in my life right now to make it whole. He told me when I was coming here that you knew him. He told me you might not be supportive of us because he dated your best friend prior to getting help. I know recently he reached out to her to say sorry. It's part of the program. We have to make amend with those we hurt from our own suffering we did in silence. I hope she can forgive him. He's not that guy, I promise." Who was she talking to like this? I know what type of guy he is, but abused? Josh? By whom? I was so lost in this story and shocked by what she was telling me I almost laughed. I had to bite my cheeks to hold back the laughter, but that's another issue. Was she really buying into this? Josh abused? The white preppy boy who came from money and was successful before graduating high school. The same Josh who spoiled my friend with lavish gifts and lies. The same Josh whose parents never missed a game or ceremony and screamed his name from the bleachers, so everyone knew that was their pride and joy. I didn't know what to say! "Oh, wow, I am so sorry, Jessica, for all the pain you endured, and I am glad you have someone like Josh to help you through it. I really hope for your sake you are right, and he has changed. Like I said, just be careful."

After I finished with Mrs. Robins and Jessica, I took a second to text Kay before my next client. *"Kay Kay, we need to talk! Text me when you are off. I will come by."* First, I need to know if Josh apologized, and second, I need to tell her Jessica is Mrs. Robins's granddaughter. I can't believe he has come up with such an elaborate scheme as to claim he was abused. Man, his game is getting better. Playing girls on a new level. I mean, a part of me is actually impressed. I should've given him more credit back in the day.

15

Kayla

I finished my shift on my first day back at work since my mom has been released from the hospital, and I am literally feeling the anxiousness of having to go home. I do not want to leave work. I was hoping to pick up another shift. Anything to avoid my mother and her toxic addiction. I decided that maybe just leaving her a note would be the best decision instead of chatting with her about leaving. I know she needs help, but if she's not going to try to help herself, I can't be held responsible for her actions. I am over trying to save the person she has become. I don't think I can take one more night of hell with her, and after reading my contract from the apartment I put a deposit on, I see I will not get my money back if I back out now. The money isn't the issue as much as dealing with my mom's shenanigans. I just can't do it anymore. I have been so preoccupied I haven't responded to any texts or checked any social media. My mom takes over my entire life. Last night was another episode of hell. She left the house on foot and told me she was walking to her friends' house. I wasn't aware she had any friends. I decided to follow her, and when she arrived a few blocks away from home, she called out to a man I presumed named Paul. She was slurring her words so bad it was hard to tell what she was saying, but my guess was correct to an extent. Apparently, she refers to him as Pauly.

Paul or Pauly lives in a duplex a few blocks from our home. His house was dirty. It reminded me of a hoarder's house because the outside was a disaster. There was overgrown grass, a broken metal gate, and the house was covered in what looked like mold. The front porch had old toys that a child must have played with years ago. It was awful. I watched as my mom staggered up the sidewalk and then the steps of the front porch. She banged on the door, still slurring her words as she screamed for "Pwalee, I know you huuurr meeeee… Pwaw-wleee." Finally, a rough-looking man who was nothing but a skeleton came to the door with no shirt on and ripped-up jeans. When he began talking to her, I noticed he was missing his teeth. He moved to let her in, and the door slammed behind them. I stood there for a minute, thinking my mom has really hit rock bottom if this was a man she was dating. I decided to take a picture of the house and get the address. I sent the picture to my uncle Rodney along with the location. He responded that he was familiar with Paul Ruben, and she was fine. I was confused and asked him how he could say that. Did he look at the house and the yard? He told me Paul has been in trouble with the law several times, his home was a place he has visited frequently, and to go on home because he would pick her up later. I am really starting to get annoyed by how much my mom's brother defends her poor choices in people. He defends her every move like she can do no wrong. It makes zero sense. This was another confirmation I had to move out. That night around eleven pm, my uncle's cruiser pulled into the driveway, hauling a sick and starving Slim up to the front porch. I didn't even budge this time to help him. I knew the drill by now. He will leave, and I will be left to care for her. My face burned with red blood flushing into my veins. I could feel the heat of anger rise up inside of me. I was so sick of this shit. I felt the tears well up in my eyes, and I tried to swallow the lump in my throat, but it was not going away. I stood there with tears streaming down my face listening to my uncle tell me she would be okay and to take good care of her, she was a good person, and I should know that it was not her fault. I hated him for this! I hated him for always having her back like she was some kind of prize to be won. He protected her at all costs. I know he saw my flushed face and tears, but of course, he ignored my pain and tended to his irrational sister. I rolled my eyes at each one of his sentences. By the time he left, I was past the point of my blood boiling. I didn't even care what happened! I ran to my room and slammed my door shut. She was not my responsibility, and this could not keep happening day in and day out. I cried myself to sleep only to be awoken at two am to my mother throwing up in my room next to my bed. I literally lay in my bed begging God to take her! Just take her, please, just take her! I was so frustrated! I had to work the morning shift at eight am, and here she was, puking her guts out right next to me. I got up and screamed at her. I said the most awful things, and in all my life, I have never talked to my mother like that. I didn't give her a shower this time. Instead, I huffed and puffed my angry breaths and threw her on the couch! I scrubbed my floor clean and headed for Jerimiah's room. It wreaked so bad in mine I couldn't take it! I opened my bedroom window and put the fan on, but I knew it would be awhile before that smell evaporated. I slept in J's bed, and it made me realize how much I missed him. When I woke up this morning, I sent him another quick text to tell him I loved him and that I was moving out. I think a part of me is hoping he will come back and live with me. We can start over and be the brother and sister we never got to be thanks to our declining mother. My hopes were quickly crushed when he responded on my way into work, saying, "*Good for you, K.*" That was it. Just a couple of words to remind me my brother is gone and not just because we have miles between us, but he is gone altogether from his past!

~

As I pulled up to my house, I saw Niv's car, and my heart sank. I completely forgot she texted me that we needed to talk. The thing about my life is, I can't always be a good friend because I am too busy raising my grown mother. I know I will have to deal with her, and she is going to go off on a tangent about how I never hit her back and it was important and blah blah. I am so not in the mood for this. I sit in my car, trying to prepare myself for what I am about to walk into. I can't even think about anything other than where my mom is and who is picking her up and what time she will pass out and how I can avoid her. I know it's unfair, but Niv never had a life like mine, so she doesn't get it. What she considers important is never on the same scale as mine.

I unbuckled my seatbelt and let it slide back to its place. I turned off the car and pulled the key from the ignition. Just as I was opening my car door, I heard her. "OMG, girl, I have been trying to get a hold of you for days. I really need to tell you something, Kay. You're going to want to hear this, I promise." All I can do to respond is,

"Niv, is my mom home?"

She looks at me crazy and says, "No, girl, she's probably at the bar," as if it is a joke to her. I think most people view it that way. They make jokes to downplay it and make it funny, so no one actually investigates the real truth of what I deal with. This is how people deal with circumstances; they literally pretend they are not happening, and that makes them feel better. I, on the other hand, do deal with it. I have to deal with it every day! I appease her and pour us both some Coke and add a shot of Captain to take the edge off. We sit at the bar in my kitchen with nothing but the dining room light on. Our house is small, and my dining room is basically part of my kitchen. The table is inches away from the kitchen counter. It's pretty dark, and I just wish it was quiet too. That is not going to be the case, unfortunately, because Nivea has found me.

"Okay, Niv, tell me what the big story is you have to get out." She is overly ecstatic, of course, with way too much energy at this time of night.

"Okay, so remember Mrs. Robins?" I nod my head because of course I do. The whole town knows her. She continues with the anticipation for my reaction to the bomb she is about to drop. "Well, she came to the shop the other day, and there was someone driving her car, and she wanted me to do the driver's hair, and Kay, when I looked, it was Jessica, like Jessica as in Josh's Jessica. That is her granddaughter. Remember when we found out from Facebook, she moved up here to live with her grandmother? Well, apparently..."

I cut her off mid-sentence, "Oh, shoot! Oh my God! I completely forgot!"

"Forgot what?"

I was unsure of whether to share this information with her, but I did anyway. "Josh just texted me the other day. Well, not texted but hit me up on Facebook Messenger, and I never even opened it. He probably thinks I am ignoring him, but I have been so busy with my mom that I completely forgot about it."

Nivea couldn't wait for her turn to talk, which pretty much summed up all conversations with Niv.

"WAIT! Let me finish telling you. I know what the message says." Now I am all for listening to this, but in my mind, I am thinking, Niv, how the hell do you know what my private message from Josh says unless you read it? "So, Jessica told me she met Josh in Miami at a retreat for abused victims. Can you believe this crock of shit he used to game her? Okay, just wait, it gets better. So, he has to complete some sort of step process where you ask for forgiveness or some shit, and he sent you a message to say sorry. Hahahahaha, can you believe that? Like he is really trying to get this girl to believe that he was abused and is sorry for how he treated you. Josh has never been sorry to anyone for anything in his life and abused? Hahahaha, I was trying to keep a straight face the whole time, but man, it was tough. You and I both know preppy perfectionist did not get abused. He really got her believing it, though, and now she thinks they are helping each other cope with her REAL abuse and his pretend abuse."

I sat there in silence. I couldn't believe it. Was Josh abused, and I missed all the signs? Was I not there for him? Why didn't he talk to me? Why didn't he come to me and tell me? I felt awful. I felt sick and like I owed him an apology. My heart broke for him, and I could see Niv was all too happy to share this, but a part of me knows Josh intimately, and she doesn't, so I felt like I had to read his message in private and she needed to leave.

"Niv, I am sorry, but I really am too tired for a night of drinking and bashing Josh. I honestly have had the roughest past few days with my mom, and I just want to go to bed. Can we maybe pick this up another time?" I know my best friend, and this was not what she wanted to hear. She was not happy I just ended her gossip streak. She looked at me like I was the rudest person she ever met, slammed her glass down, and basically told me, "Yea, we can catch up another time," but the tone of her voice let me know she was pissed. People are like that, though. If you don't give them the reaction they want, they get really uptight. Niv felt like she was passing me the gold, and I should have been grateful for her investigation, but I can't deal with her putting Josh down right now. What if it was true? What if he was abused? I was in disbelief I didn't notice, and then I felt even more guilty. He probably didn't think he could share that with me since I was always concerned with my own problems—my mother. UGH! Just another thing she ruined and took from me. I decided to take a long hot shower and climb into bed without eating. I was too upset to eat.

Lying in my bed with the fan blasting on high and candles burning all around me to deter me from the smell that will forever be a nose punch in my room, I decide to read Josh's message. I open my messenger app and click on his name.

"Kayla, how are you? I know it's weird to hear from me, and you may not even open this message or respond, which is fine, but I had to send this for me. I messed up a lot when we were a couple, and I was not a good guy to you. I realize that now, and after a lot of therapy, I have worked through my own indiscretions, and I realize how awful I was. I'm not sure why you loved me or put up with me back then, but I need you to know I am truly sorry. You didn't deserve the man I was to you, and I know I can't go back in time to change that, but going forward, I hope you can forgive me. Take care, Kay!"

I read the message over and over and over again. I couldn't take my eyes off the message and its words. There was no way Josh was lying to this Jessica chick. He obviously was really hurt, and I had no idea. Instead of listening to him and trying to help him, I just worried about me and played the victim role. This message brought back feelings I really tried to tuck away. I felt this strong urge to reply that I still loved him, and I missed him so much, and I was moving out and leaving my mom, and we should start over and try again. I didn't, though. I chose to keep it simple.

"Hey Josh! How are you? I really appreciate you sending this message, and of course, I forgive you. I never had any ill feelings towards you. I hope you know that. Please reach out to me anytime. I'd love to hear from you more often. Xoxo"

I sent the message before I got trapped overthinking it. I lay in my bed just staring at my phone, willing it to light up with a notification that Josh responded. I don't know what I expected; he has a girlfriend and a new life now that doesn't include me, but a small part of me really wants him back. When things were good, they were really good. Those are the times I like to remember. Since I had no mother to care for tonight, I rolled over and closed my eyes to silence. Morning would be here far too soon, and I desperately needed the rest.

16

Jerimiah

Keith was standing in the kitchen, making us each a cup of coffee, and I couldn't help but stare at his masculine physique. He was extraordinarily beautiful. Everything about this man was perfection. I watched him shirtless and wearing nothing but a pair of loose shorts as he poured creamer in the cups. When he turned a cup in each hand to walk towards the bedroom, I met his eyes, and he smiled.

"Buenos dias, mi amor." I loved when he spoke Spanish to me. I smiled back and kissed him ever so slightly on his pouty wet lips. He handed me my coffee, and we sat down on the new couch we just purchased. Together, we held each other, drinking our coffee and sitting in silence. The only sound was our breathing and the rhythm of his heartbeat pounding in my ear as my head lay on his chest. The last time I felt this happy had to be before my father died when I had an actual mom. I think about them from time to time and how things are going in Florida. As I lie here with Keith, I tell him my sister is moving out. I explain how she texted me that it was time to go. Keith asks me if I am happy about this and how I feel. To be honest, I am happy my sister finally decided to do something for herself and not revolve her life around my mom. I've told Keith all about my mom and the issues I've had growing up without a father, a neglectful mother, and a burden sister. He had a completely different upbringing. Keith is super close to his family. They are very much the family you see on TV that you wish you could have in real life but know it's not possible. He calls his parents every day. They love him no matter what he does because their love is unconditional. He grew up Catholic, and his parents raised him that being gay is unacceptable, but when he came out to them, they welcomed the news with open arms. I couldn't imagine what that would be like. To have support from my family about my sexuality, yea, right. He never had to hide who he was. His mother always repeats, "You hate the sin but love the sinner." She tells me the same. She is very warm and loving but does advise that the way of life we live is not what Jesus intended; however, His love is unconditional, and we have already been forgiven for our sins. He died on the cross for us. She tells Keith the same way Jesus loves her, and her mistakes are forgiven, so are his. Her love is unconditional, just like Jesus' love. She told me one day that unconditional love means to love without conditions. There are no limits or restrictions to love. I wouldn't know. My family has every type of restriction you can imagine. They are strong Republicans, and they have no love for blacks, gays, or anything other than a white man with a rifle ready to shoot. I never felt like I fit in with my own family. I never really wanted to fit in with them either. Their beliefs were never my own. I couldn't hate people for their skin color, and the biggest reason I think Kay and I don't have a bond is that she followed suit with them. She jumped into formation like a robot. Kay never dared step out of line or say no. She did as she was told. I wanted a sister, and I needed a mom, but instead, I got neither. My only solace was on my birthday each year. It was one year closer to moving out. I want to come out to my family, but I also feel I don't owe it to them. I really don't care what they think or how they feel because I already know their take on my decision. I'm not ready to put myself through that. One day, though, I am going to tell them. I am going to walk in and boast and brag about my boyfriend and our love. One day, I am going to make them see the real me. One day, but not any time soon.

Keith left his imprint on the couch to take a shower, and I stayed lying there soaking up his warmth and smell. I grabbed my iPhone and decided to see what was new on Facebook. I chose to keep all my personal life private from my family; thank God for this option on Facebook. It's like I live a secret life. I see my sister has posted nothing, and I am not surprised; she was never one for social media anyways. I do notice Nivea posting all her new hair pics, and I clicked the heart because I've always felt she was super talented. I saw one picture of a makeover, and I almost choked on my own spit! No way! It was my sister. She actually got purple streaks in her hair! Not just streaks, but my sister got purple! This was something. I had to comment. It was killing me. *"Kayla, I cannot believe you let Nivea put PURPLE in your hair! I absolutely love it, and you look beautiful as ever. Nivea, you did your thing, girl."*

~

Keith, fresh from taking a shower, sat beside me on the couch. I showed him the picture of my sister's new hair, and he agreed it was perfect for her. We both sat there talking about what to do today and decided on Oakland. We opted to take the ferry. The thing about the Bay area is the weather is much cooler than the weather in Florida. We never experience severe thunderstorms or raging humidity. The weather stays pretty cool and breezy, especially at night. It's easy to make plans when you have little to no worries about inclement weather. We both wore pullover hoodies for our ferry ride since the ocean breeze can be quite chilling. Something I now enjoy, like a rainbow after the storm.

As we rode the ferry to Oakland, I stared out at the ocean, taking in the picturesque views. I stared at Keith and thought about how lucky I was to have found him. As I looked around the ferry, I noticed a family sitting together in the middle. The son was sitting by his mom and what appeared to be his boyfriend. They were laughing and joking, having a good old time. I smiled at them with a huge smile of love and approval. I couldn't turn my head out of both jealousy and happiness. Eventually, I gave in and looked at Keith, and he looked back at me and smiled. I looked back out to the ocean, and as the salty breeze washed over my face, I thought I have to tell them. I am not going to tell my family I am gay, not because I feel that I owe it to them, but because I want to let go of negativity. I no longer want to hide who I am. If it means losing the people I care about, that will be hard, I cannot deny, but at the end of the day, I have to do this for myself. I owe it to Keith and myself to be honest about us. I have this confidence now that I never possessed before. I feel brave and vulnerable all at the same time. It's weird because I have no idea how this will turn out; however, I can't help but assume the worst. Anything other than that would be a step above in the right direction. I can't decide if I should go home or do it over the phone, but I thought if I am going to do this, I should do it face to face. Introduce Keith and walk with my head held high. *This is the man I want to be with, Mom and Kay. I don't know if you will accept him, but I don't care. I am not asking you to accept him or me for who I really am. I just wanted to tell you I am gay, and Keith and I are a couple. We live together in San Fran, and I lied about school.* That is pretty much all I think I will tell them. Short, sweet, and simple. They can take it or leave it, but right now, I just want it out in the open.

"Keith, would you be willing to fly home to Lutz with me to tell my family we are a couple?"

Keith looked at me with his sweet face glowing in the sun, "Yea, if you're sure that is what you want to do, you know I will be there for you. I will always be there for you."

I knew he would, and with that, I grabbed his arm, leaned my head on his shoulder, and whispered, "I know." I can't stop loving this man. I can't pretend anymore. I am finally ready to tell them.

When we got back from Oakland, I decided to pull out my laptop and start looking for flights. I knew I needed to request time off at work, so I decided before I put in for my PTO (paid time off), I should see when the best time is to fly financially. Booking two flights from California to Florida wasn't going to be cheap, and I needed to make sure it fit our budget. I used Google Flights since I heard from coworkers it was the best site for an affordable flight, and I found two tickets for $900 round trip. We would leave next weekend, so I literally had one week to inform my job. Keith agreed to purchase the flights before the price skyrocketed. I clicked the *Buy Flight* button and input my credit card information as fast as I could. I hit *Submit*, and when the email confirmation came through, I felt the nerves rising in my chest. I can't believe I am doing this. Finally, I am taking my life into my own hands and being who I was truly meant to be. I sat there for a minute, staring at my computer screen in awe of my flight confirmation. Then it hit me, should I tell Kay I am coming? I wonder if I should look for a place to stay. I have not decided if this will be a surprise or not. I grabbed my phone, thinking I should at least give the heads up, but then I thought better of it. Due to the reason for the visit, I don't want to create a lot of joy that I am coming home. I will just show up with Keith and play it by ear.

17

Nivea

I pulled up to the Levitts' house, all excited because finally, Miranda's mom agreed to let us read the diary. We hopefully find some interesting stuff in there. I am also happy to be off and hanging out with Miranda because we owe each other nothing. We just met, and there is no past to bind us together or bring about any drama or awkward feelings. I need a friend like that after my last encounter with Kayla because I try to be a loyal good friend to everyone in my life, but Kay gets put at the top of that list, and she seems so ungrateful for it. I hate that she doesn't reciprocate it or just say thank you. It makes me not want to share information with her. Like why I care so much if she doesn't even care. After all, it is her life, not mine. Either way, I think I might fall back for a little bit. Kay seems like she needs to take some time to herself and get her shit together. She uses her mom as a viable excuse for everything, and she always has. It's convenient for her. She stays in the same house, at the same job, and never plans to leave because why would she? That's not the Kay way. Right now, I am happy to just be here with Miranda and not have to deal with Kay and all her bull. Besides, Miranda and I get along really well. I may never see her again once she leaves Lutz, so I have no ties to worry me.

I walked up the old sidewalk to the run-down old front porch and saw the door was open. Odd, because it is too damn hot in this humid weather to leave the door open. I pulled the screen door back and walked in.

"Hey, hey! It's me, Niv!"

I heard Miranda yell, "Hey, girl, we are back here! Come on back to the kitchen."

As I walked through the house, it seemed quite warm, and I thought, did the AC break? I can't be here if the AC broke. I started to feel beads of sweat on my forehead, and when I reached the kitchen, I saw both Ran and her mom sitting at the table.

"Hey y'all, listen, it is hot as hell up in here. Did the AC break? I am already sweating."

Miranda's mom looked at me, and with a wipe of sweat from her own head, she said, "Yes, the guy will be here soon. We called an HVAC guy a while ago. He said to give him two hours, and we were hoping he would have been here by now." I was not expecting to attend a sweat fest today, but here I am,

I guess. I see they are not doing anything but looking through old photos at the table and drinking glasses of cool lemonade. I gather myself and get a glass of the iced drink to at least cool my throat. I am not going to make it in here. I sit down in the faux leather chair at the table, only to notice my legs sticking to the seat immediately from how hot I am.

"So, I assume you called the HVAC guy to rush him, right? Let him know this is a Florida summer and we need air?"

Miranda smiled and then laughed. "Nivea, you will be okay; you were born here. Help us look through these photos. Maybe you recognize some of these people." I grabbed a stack of the thrown-about pictures and started skimming through them. I couldn't believe it, but there were people I actually knew. As a matter of fact, Mrs. Levitt's old ass even had photos from an old Christmas event that took place here in Lutz. I wasn't even born yet, and I know this because I see my mom's fresh baby face standing in downtown. I smiled at the picture glaring with delight. My mother was beautiful in her teens. She looked so happy, and I thought about how much I miss her and really need to reach out to my parents.

Sitting in this heat is excruciating, but it's not as noticeable when you are looking at photos and going through boxes of albums that bring back memories you didn't have. I don't exactly know my parents prior to my birth, but I fondly remember their stories, and seeing the stories come to life in these photos is like having a memory I didn't know existed. I can now put a real picturesque view into focus instead of the made-up one in my head. While looking through several albums, I find one in particular with newspaper clippings. I look at the title, and it reads *Lutz Resident's Remains Found Today on Turtle Drive*. Oh, it's Kayla's father! I gasped and grabbed my mouth but didn't realize it at the moment until both Miranda and her mom jumped up and asked if I was okay.

"Yes, I am fine, sorry, it just caught me off guard. My best friend Kayla, who I told you about, this is her father's murder. It went unsolved, and it's a cold case today. I've never seen all these newspaper articles because we were just ten at the time of his murder. I just remember everyone talking about it. It sent so much fear through our little town. Everyone assumed it was a black man from Tampa. No one around here likes blacks. I was never sure about it being anyone from Tampa. I just couldn't figure out why Kayla's uncle, Rodney, couldn't solve it."

Miranda's mom grabbed the album with me and looked at the articles. "Oh my God, I remember this. I remember my mom becoming obsessed. She went on and on about it. No one had ever been murdered here before. She was determined to follow the case and know what happened. You know, my mom always thought it was strange that no one in the police department took it more seriously. She said they should have alerted people from the FBI or somewhere they were used to solving murders. She felt they had no experience here in Lutz and that the person who did it was probably living among us."

I sat back in my chair and thought about what she just said. What if the person who murdered Kayla's dad did live right here in Lutz? What if the person was someone we knew? I got super hype about this. I was ready to go all detective and pretend I was on an episode of CSI. I couldn't be happier to hear this, and it had me thinking we haven't read the diary yet. We needed to read that and see if her opinion of what happened was in there. Could you imagine someone right here in Lutz! A murderer! I wondered if it was a pastor or, even better, a schoolteacher. This was thrilling to me; I am obsessed with crime shows; this right here was my new hobby. Solve murder! Miranda's mom took the newspaper articles in the photo album and started flipping through them one by one until she landed on, she read aloud,

"CASE OF TONY GRAY CLOSED – MURDER NOT SOLVED

In the small town of Lutz, Florida, a thirty-seven-year-old man had disappeared. The man was working for Tampa Financial at the time as a Bank Manager. He served several banks across the United States and ran one of the most successful branches in all of Florida. Tampa financial has several sister banks that Mr. Gray handled, along with being a shareholder with all partners. When he did not show up for work on the 9th of October, several alarms were raised by his coworkers. Jackson Knight of West Morro Bank in Tennessee said, 'We had a conference call that day at eight am, and Tony was never late. He would be the first one on the call welcoming everyone. When he wasn't there, and we hadn't heard from him, we knew something was wrong. Tony would never miss an important call; it just wasn't who he was as a boss. He took his role seriously.' Tony Gray was never late to work, according to colleagues. He stayed late and traveled all the time to keep the business afloat. He was a great man to work for and created a moral that most businesses would envy. Mr. Gray was married with two children, a boy and a girl. The family lived in Lutz, just twenty or so minutes outside of Tampa. His wife Joanna Gray stated she hadn't heard from him since the night before. Neighbors were interviewed but stated that nothing out of the ordinary took place. That Sunday night, his wife explained that they went out to a nice dinner at McClintocks. She stated that after dinner, they took a walk on the beach and then headed for home. She realized they were out of milk and the children would need it for breakfast. She told The Press that she asked Tony to go out and get milk. After drinking all night, she was exhausted and decided to go to bed. When she woke up that morning to get the kids ready, she realized Tony hadn't brought milk home. She figured he probably fell asleep on the couch and then headed off for work early since it was Monday and Tony always went in early after a weekend. It wasn't until her phone rang and one of the branch employees was asking if Tony was there. Mrs. Gray did some small conferences for local news asking people to turn over any evidence or information they have on Tony. The family set up a small reward of 10,000 dollars for any valid information leading to the disappearance of Tony Gray. Unfortunately, that following Tuesday, a woman walking her dog along Turtle Drive came across a bone. She told police her dog ran off and kept barking, and by the time she caught up to him, he was chewing on something that looked like a

human bone. She told the police her fear was it could be Tony,
but she was hoping it was from an animal. The police in Lutz
headed up the investigation shutting down Turtle Drive.
Rodney Alser was the one who led the investigation, which
many thought odd as he was a fairly new detective at the
time. There were other seasoned detectives that many residents
thought best to investigate such a horrific event, but Rodney
Alser stated it was his brother-in-law and he wanted the case.
The body was found in the North area of Turtle Pond. It was
assumed that crocodiles might have attacked the body because
one arm and half the face were missing upon arrival. The
body had started to decay from the heat in October. This was
not unusual as it's hot all year in the Tampa Bay area. Upon
further investigation, it was obvious the victim had multiple
gunshot wounds. The murder weapon was determined to be
a nine-millimeter. At that time, there was little DNA to go
off of. Now, after many interviews and little evidence, the
case is being closed due to insufficient information. This will
remain not only the first missing person's case but also the
first murder for Lutz. This will remain their one and only
unsolved murder as talk of reopening the case was denied by
the new sheriff, who was also the related brother-in-law that
initially investigated the case three years prior, Rodney Alser.
Gray's family couldn't bear the truth of the murder and chose
to move away. We reached out to them, but they declined to
be interviewed for this article."

I just sat there and couldn't speak. It hit me like a ton of
bricks. Wow, we really did only have one murder, and it was
my best friend's dad. My best friend had no dad or grandpar-
ents or any family other than her effed mom, who gets drunk

every night. My best friend had to deal with this knowledge of her father being shot and ripped apart by a gator. Her father was left in a swamp like a piece of trash, and when the opportunity to reopen the case came about, no one was interested. Kay would've been thirteen then. How come I don't remember a second attempt at reopening the case? I wonder why I don't remember us talking about this or how she felt or why they denied it. I couldn't help but wonder what that must have been like for Kay and Jerimiah. Her dad was splattered across newspapers and became the center of attention for any media in our area. Her dad was dead, and he was murdered, and no one knew why or who did it. I can't believe this never bothered me before. Miranda looked at me and asked if I was okay. I assured I was and that it just brought back memories. This was true, just not entirely. I felt sick, and the damn heat was making me feel worse. Where was the AC guy? Miranda brought over her grandmother's diary and opened it up to start skimming.

"Hey, maybe something about the murder is in here. I mean, clearly, my grandmother was obsessed with Tony Gray."

I swallowed my spit and let out a huge amount of air. Apparently, I was holding my breath without realizing it. I had to brace myself for what she might read. I was still processing the newspaper article and the broken AC.

∼

Miranda read through the pages and finally looked up and screamed, "LISTEN TO THIS! Grandma must've thought the family did it. She wrote in her diary that she thinks they were involved. She has a whole story here about how she went down to the station and met with Rodney, the detective on the case and felt like he was hiding something. She even spoke to his wife Joanna, and rumor has it he had another baby. A love child! Apparently, he had an affair, and Grandma thinks that the affair and the baby are the reason for his death. She says here on one page that while talking to Joanna in a drunken state, she slipped up and stated that the little bitch Tiffany who lives in Chicago better never come around here wanting to meet her siblings. OH MY GOD! This means your friend Kayla has a…"

I cut her off and screamed out loud, "SISTER!" Holy shit! What do I do with this information? Is this true? Wait, I can't even think. I can't even process what I just heard. How could I not know? How could any of us not know? What does Kay know? What if she has always known? Okay, okay, I got to calm down. It is far too hot to be getting all worked up. I asked her to read more and see if we can find out any information on Tiffany. I grabbed my phone and searched Facebook for 'Tiffany Gray, Chicago,' and so many people came up. I needed help to narrow down my search. Wait, here it is. Her mother's name is Seven Moore. I searched a Seven Moore, and then there it was; she popped right up. Her name now was Seven Moore Lyons. I saw she lived in Chicago, Illinois, and her daughter was clearly her everything. Tiffany Gray Lyons. Holy Shit! I almost fell out of the sticky hot chair! Tiffany and her mom are black!

Before I could think or say another word about this, there was a man on the front porch yelling, "Anybody home? My name's Ted, here to fix the air." Some people have awful timing. I would normally complain about that or would have said come back later, but this heat was brutal, and I needed air to think. Miranda's mom ran to the door to let Ted in and led him to the unit in the house where the main vent was under the thermostat. I sat at the small table, eyes wide as can be, just staring at Miranda. I can't believe Kayla has a black sister. I repeated it over and over and over until I finally started laughing hysterically. This was some shit right here. This was going to be the talk of the town, and it's only Monday! I wonder what else old Mrs. Levitt was hiding in this diary of hers!

18

Kayla

Today's tasks seem to never end. I have been all over trying to set up cable, turn on electricity, order furniture, hire movers, and buy all the stuff I need for an apartment. I am kind of freaking out about this major change I am making, but another part of me is feeling more secure and confident than ever. I went to Hobby Lobby and grabbed the cutest décor ever. My little bathroom will be lots of bright oranges. I chose a starfish theme since it's fitting for Florida. I wanted something to spruce it up since I chose a dark gray and blush living room. My couch is a beautiful charcoal color, and it has two recliners, one on each end of the loveseat. I picked out pillows with a chevron pattern that are gray, blush, and white. My coffee table is glass with silver legs, and I found the most perfect fake flowers at Hobby

Lobby with a beautiful vase to put in the center. I opted for sheer curtains to allow lots of light and did a gray twisted curtain at the top for added design. My kitchen is going to be blue like the ocean. I found the best pots and pans I could for the low at Target and added a few plates and silverware to match. I think the kitchen will complement my living room perfectly. I do not have space for a table, but I do have a bar, so I purchased two bar stools that are blue leather from Rooms to Go. Since I have no bedroom in my studio apartment, I purchased a blow-up mattress just in case I want to use it or have someone over. Maybe Jerimiah will come home and want to stay with me. I just wanted to have one on hand. I will be sleeping on my new super comfortable couch. It's extra plush, and when I recline back, I feel like I am lying in a bed. It goes so far! The apartment is mine come Saturday, and I am trying to gather up what I need for move-in day. My room is in boxes and looks like a mess. I am going through all my stuff, stuff I haven't seen for years in my closet, and I come across a card from my dad. It was just before he died. He bought me a card because I had a bad day at school. Kids were making fun of me for wanting to dress up as a baseball player zombie for Halloween. I will never forget that day. I came home crying and ran to my room. I sat on my bed with my hands holding my face in my lap, just devasted. My dad came home early that night, and when he came to see me, he could tell I had been crying. He took me out for ice cream that night, just the two of us. When I woke up the next morning, I had a card that read, 'Be who you were meant to be, because I love whoever that person is, and I always will.' Inside, he wrote me a note, "My dearest Kayla, I want you to know that you can be whoever and whatever you want in life. Sometimes people will not like your choices, but stand behind them and never give up without a fight." As I read the card, tears filled my eyes. I missed him more now than ever. I needed him to tell me it was okay to move out and to stand behind this decision and that Mom would be okay and I was not abandoning her. I have a tremendous amount of guilt for wanting to leave. I held the card to my chest and cried. I couldn't stop crying. I was hurting like it happened yesterday. I felt empty, and I wanted to make the pain stop. My heart ached for my dad and all of his advice and love. I would give anything to have him back.

I quickly wiped my face and put the photo away when I heard the screen door slam. I jumped up to see who it was, and of course, it was my mother. She was half sober and talking about some woman who disrespected her at the grocery store. I could only imagine what the clerk's story was compared to my mother's. I walked down the short hallway to our kitchen and saw her standing at the stove, lighting a cigarette.

"Hey, Mom."

She looked up and inhaled a puff of smoke that she slowly exhaled while staring at me. "Aren't you supposed to be at work or something?"

I wasn't even sure how to answer that since I haven't told her yet that I am moving out. I decided it was now or never.

"No, actually, I am packing up my things. I'm moving out on Saturday. I found a nice studio apartment downtown."

She didn't even flinch. I was nervous by how silent she was, just puffing her cigarette and not saying a word. Finally, she looked up at me and then ashed her cigarette in the sink. I stood so still you could have painted me.

"Well, I guess it's for the better. I don't need nobody around here telling me what to do all day and night. You ain't much help no way, always working and telling me I need rehab. I'm glad you and your brother will be gone. Now I don't have to feed nobody but me!"

I was a bit confused by her remarks. She hasn't bought food or cooked for Jerimiah and me in twelve years or more. She was in no way a mother who took care of her children and stayed home worrying where we were. I guess this was her way of dealing with the fact that her children were leaving her. I walked towards her and put my arms around her, making sure to not burn myself with the lit end of her cigarette that was practically gone. She put one arm around me, and then I whispered, "I love you, Mom," and with that, I kissed her cheek and let her go.

I returned to my room to continue packing while she sat watching TV, and I knew she probably passed out from pulling an all-nighter and day drinking. My mom had a very routine schedule; I always knew where I could find her and what she would be doing. As I was packing listening to Taylor Swift's Pandora Radio, I got a text from Nivea. I felt awful because the last time we spoke, I was not genuinely nice to her. I opened the messaging app and read the longest text I think she has ever sent me.

"Kay, listen, we have to talk. I don't care how busy you are or if you want to be alone or whatever you got going on. This is serious! It's about your dad. I think you need to know some things, and I'm not sure how you will take them, but I have news that is going to change your life. Also, you need to get in touch with Jerimiah. He should know the news, and then the two of you should talk. LMK when ur free."

I had to read this text multiple times to make sure I understood it correctly. Nivea was not one for lengthy messages. I normally got one or two words. This was crazy. I had a lot going on already with moving, and now this. I was hoping that it was just another one of Niv's ploys to start some drama. However, a big part of me knew that when it came to my father's death, Niv would never play games. What she did recently with Josh was just Niv being Niv, but this seemed different and genuine. Why would I need to contact Jerimiah? I took a deep breath and decided to text back, *"Hey, I'm off today. Are you around? I can meet you now."*

I waited to see her reply, and it came right through, *"Come to my shop."* Now, this response was a normal type Niv text. I figured it couldn't be too serious if I was going to the shop. She wouldn't put my business out there to her clients. I got up and changed my clothes really quickly to look suitable in public and then grabbed my keys and left.

19

Nivea

After yesterday's craziness, I decided I couldn't hang on to my newfound information, and I needed to tell Kayla immediately. What she will do with it I don't know, but I have to tell her. I opened my shop early this morning because I was booked solid, and now that I finally finished my last client, I decided to text Kay and give her the heads up we need to talk. I am pacing the floors back and forth in my shop, and not because I am nervous to tell her, but well, yea, I am nervous to tell her. I wasn't raised to be like everyone else. My parents were hippies, and they didn't agree with the life of Lutz. The people here are racist and see one side of every story, the white side. Kayla may be my best friend, but we have vastly different viewpoints. The topic never really comes into view because it's not one either of us brings up. I date a man based on his priorities. I need a man who is hard working like myself and has a business-oriented mindset but knows how to have fun. The color of their skin or their background is not necessarily important to me. There were times we went out in Tampa, and I hooked up with Puerto Rican guys on the dance floor, and Kayla made a scene by excusing my actions and chalking them up to one too many shots. The thing is, I was never drunk; I found them attractive but never felt the need to go there with her. It's hard to explain to someone who doesn't understand, or who doesn't want to understand, for that matter. I grabbed my energy drink and took a sip when I heard my doorbell go off, alerting me someone has walked in. I knew it had to be Kay. I took a deep breath and walked up front.

"Niv, what's this all about? I was completely caught off guard by your text. How did you find out some information about my dad? Who told you and why? What's this got to do with J?" She was bombarding me with questions, and I was like, okay, Niv, you gotta just tell her. Just come out with it. I told her it was best she sits down, and she told me no. I understood her fear and agitation because she was in a vulnerable position.

"Kay, listen, I am sorry to tell you this because I know you are not going to understand it or maybe not even believe it…"

"NIVEA, WHAT IS IT?"

I could tell she was losing patience, so I blurted it out. "Your dad had an affair, and you have an older sister, and she lives in Chicago. And that's not all; she's black." I stood there, afraid for a second that she might hit me. She wasn't saying a word, and then, out of nowhere, she sat down in a salon chair and started cracking up. Now, this was unexpected. I was happy to see her laughing, so I joined in. As I was laughing, I looked over at her and asked what was so funny.

She literally smacked my arm and was like, "I thought something serious happened, Niv. You scared me," and she kept on laughing. Now I am not a detective, but at this point, I am wondering if she is drunk or just losing it.

"Kayla, look at me, I am not joking. I have proof. I found her on Facebook. I can give you all her information. She's a doctor. Your dad cheated on your mom and got this woman named Seven pregnant. She had the baby and named her Tiffany Gray. I found the information while helping Miranda at Mrs. Levitt's house. She apparently saved all the newspaper articles and even kept a journal. Your mom was the one who told her Kay. Your mom knew all this time. I'm really sorry to dump this all on you, but I thought you should know."

Kay just sat there looking at the floor. After about five minutes, she turned to look at me with the most hateful face.

"You know what, Nivea, I don't care what you say or what proof you have. My dad wouldn't sleep with no black bitch. We don't do shit like that in my family, and especially not my father! How dare you or Mrs. Levitt tell lies about my dad after he's gone and can't defend himself. I thought you were my friend, but this crosses all types of lines, Niv. I'm leaving! I have nothing more to say to you."

I stared at my empty shop, wondering how we just went from cracking up to never speaking again. Hmm, that was strange. Not what I expected. Losing my best friend wasn't on my agenda, but I guess it added itself. I am just going to give her some time to marinate on these newfound facts. She will come around, and when she does, I will be waiting.

20

Tiffany

Tonight, I am off for the first time in what feels like years. I am ready to make the most of it by going out and having some fun. I am long overdue for a good time. I texted this guy I met in med school, Daniel Hernandez, and asked him if he wanted to grab a drink and some dinner. Daniel and I both excelled in school, and we both came from prominent backgrounds. He was at the top of the class, as was I, and therefore, we worked together on many projects. We spent a lot of time hanging out and studying for exams while eating wings, drinking beer, and watching football. I always liked Daniel. He was very family-oriented, as were most Hispanics I met. Daniel was outgoing and fun, and he understood all my struggles as a doctor. He went through hell with me. We never dated or hooked up, not because I didn't want to, but more because we were so preoccupied with becoming doctors that one-night stands weren't in the cards. I have talked to Daniel here and there since starting my residency, and of course, we have kept in touch on Facebook when we had time. Thankfully, Daniel was down to meet tonight, and we agreed on a spot in downtown. It was just a casual place, and I dressed the part but made sure to go a little overboard since I never get out. I even pulled out my knee-high black boots; they went perfectly with my low-cut blouse and tight black jeans with rips down the front. Since it was July, we didn't need jackets, and that was rare for Chicago.

I headed out of my condo with my bangles jangling all the way down the hall to the elevator. I couldn't wait to swap stories with Daniel about all the craziness becoming a doctor has brought to my life. The best part about Daniel is that he understands my crazy schedule, and we can sit and talk about our residency and how much we love what we do. He understands my hectic lifestyle and hard work. We get along really well. I haven't seen him in about four months, which makes our catch-up stories that much more interesting. Inside the elevator, a cute little face greets me. The little girl is with her mother and stares in my direction, eyeing me up and down until her mother reminds her politely not to stare. I smiled, and she proceeded to say, "But Momma, she is just so pretty." I bent down and looked her in her eyes and told her, "Thank you, but you are definitely the prettiest one on the elevator." She got super shy and smiled big enough for me to see her two front teeth were missing. When we stopped moving, I walked off first into the lobby and waved goodbye to my new friend. I cannot wait to have children of my own. I walked outside, hailed a cab and headed downtown to the restaurant.

When I arrived, Daniel was already there with two drinks in hand. I sat down next to him at the bar and took a sip of my drink. We exchanged hugs, and I expressed my gratitude for his early arrival. I hated sitting alone in a public place. It was mortifying to me. I always felt like everyone was staring at me. The fact that he was brave enough to sit alone and not be bothered made him even more attractive to me. He was dressed in a pair of dark blue jeans and a button-down collared shirt. It was red with a small emblem of a polo sign in the corner of his chest. Daniel looked amazing tonight like always. His perfectly sculpted jawline and five o'clock shadow. He smelled like a memory I wanted to hang on to for dear life. Everything about his beautiful face and well-built body was making me warm. I felt nervous all of a sudden and realized I needed more alcohol. While we were looking at our menus, I couldn't help but look at him several times and just smile. Daniel was gorgeous. I had to get my mind off him, so I brought up work. We sat and talked about our residency while we ate sushi and downed Saki bombs. The night was cool but not cold, so we decided to take a walk. The city is gorgeous at night, and the Lake Michigan looks extra blue tonight with splashes of moonlight dances on top of it. Daniel grabbed my hand and pulled me next to him.

"Tiff, I had a lot of fun tonight. I've missed hanging out with you." I felt like my heart was going to beat right through my chest. We stopped walking, and right there, with the city lights dancing on the water and people passing, Daniel put his lips on mine. I didn't want it to end. I wanted to hold on to this moment forever. I put my head on his chest and breathed in his smell. I felt safe; I felt like this was where I was supposed to be. Everything around me seemed to stop mattering. Him. This moment. That was all I could see. We stood like this for a few minutes before I finally pulled back and invited Daniel back to my condo. He looked as if he had been waiting his whole life for me to say this to him. I laughed at his excited YES and grabbed his hand. We headed to Michigan Ave to grab a cab and head back to my place. Never letting go of one another.

Once we arrived at my condo, Daniel and I got comfortable on my couch. I opened a bottle of champagne, and we sat there in the dark, drinking and holding each other. I found him attractive and flirted with him all through med school. Nothing ever came of it. I wasn't sure why now the timing felt right, but it did. He felt right; his strong body and his overly perfect smile made me feel desperate to have him. Daniel was about to know me on a personal and intimate level. I knew once I took it there, there was no going back. I grabbed his glass and placed it on the coffee table alongside my own. I stood up, grabbed his hand, and led him to my room.

~

I woke up to Daniel getting dressed, and I sat up to check the time on my phone. It was 4:30 am. I had to be at the hospital by 2:00 pm. He walked over to me and kissed me on the forehead.

"Bye, beautiful, I will text you later. I have an early shift." I smiled and blew him a kiss with my eyes still half-closed. I lay back down on my satin pillows and started kicking my legs and slamming my arms down. YES! YES! YEES! Last night was the best night of my life. Could I really do this? Date a doctor? Could this work? I wasn't sure it was possible, but I was sure I wanted to try. He was perfect, and after last night, I knew I loved everything about Dr. Daniel Hernandez. I wasn't sure if he was going to text me later, but at that moment, I didn't care. I was going to enjoy every second of my sleep and his smell on my sheets. I rolled over and started to laugh. I really did that. Me and Daniel. I couldn't stop smiling. I set my alarm to wake up at noon and call my mom. I had to fill her in about Daniel. I couldn't wait to tell her all the details of last night's rendezvous.

21

Kayla

I pulled up to my house, fuming with rage and frustration. I couldn't believe Nivea. How could she? I was confused about how any of this could be true. First of all, my father would never sleep with another woman, let alone a black woman. That would be crossing major boundaries. That is disgusting. I can't even imagine my father looking in a black woman's direction. He would never disrespect my mom like that. They loved each other. Their marriage was sacred. My father was not a cheater. I stayed in my car, trying to process all of this. I was beyond mad at Niv. How dare she! This was low even for her. I know she loves drama, but to destroy my father's reputation and disrespect him like that was going too far. I felt sick to my stomach. How could she have proof? An old lady's diary is not proof. The frustration turned to fear, and then I couldn't stop crying. I feel like I am living someone else's life right now because this cannot be mine. A sister? A black sister? Omigosh, I can't have a black sister. I can't. I will kill myself before I claim a black girl as my sister. How could this happen? The tears were so warm they started to burn my cheeks. I felt like I couldn't breathe. My whole body felt numb. There is no way! No fucking way! I punched my steering wheel over and over again. My horn was blowing each time, but I didn't even notice. I couldn't even see straight. Knock, knock, knock, I looked over to my driver's side window and saw my mom standing there smoking a cigarette. I opened the door, and she glared at me like she didn't recognize who I was.

"You okay? I heard your horn going off and thought maybe it was for me to come out." I was crying so hard I couldn't even answer her. Slim put her cigarette out and leaned in the car to help me get out. My mom had been sleeping, and this was the time of day she was practically sober so she could think clearly for all of five minutes before she left for her all-nighter at The Basement. Together, we walked to the house and took a seat inside on the couch.

"What is all this fuss about?" I was literally sobbing and trying to catch my breath and swallow all at the same time. I grabbed the box of tissues on the end table and blew my nose and wiped my face. I looked at my mom and saw her differently. I saw a hurt woman who was betrayed and drank away her sorrows. I saw a woman who needed love, and I began to cry even louder. She moved closer to me and wrapped her bony little arms around my body. I cried on her chest while she told me it would all be alright.

When I finally got myself together and had calmed down enough to speak, I got a glass of water and drank the whole thing. I felt a headache coming on and grabbed two Tylenol to numb the pain. My mother was sitting there looking at the TV and smoking her life away. I walked over to where she was sitting and took a seat on the floor.

"Mom, I have to ask you something." She looked at me and waited, "Did Daddy cheat on you?" Her face went blank. She stood up, moving me out of the way, and walked into the kitchen, where she began to pour herself a bourbon on the rocks. "Mom, please tell me the truth. Nivea said I have…"

She cut me off, "NIVEA? How the hell did Nivea come to know this?" I couldn't speak for a second because she didn't deny it. I watched her drink one cup and then pour another and down it like it was water. My mind was racing, and I felt like the walls were closing in on me.

"Mom, what do you mean how did she know this? I accused her of lying! She's lying, right? Daddy would never sleep with nigger, right? Please tell me she's lying." She took a deep breath and sighed a loud, long burst of air from her chest.

"Kayla, your daddy was no saint! He was working up at that bank, and he traveled for work and met all kinds of people. Thought he was a big shot and could do what he wanted because he was bringing home the money. I was taking care of you, kids. Your daddy made mistakes, and that bitch was one of them. Don't go running around town investigating no shit. Keep your mouth shut if you know what's good for you."

I froze in my tracks and watched her grab the whole bottle and walk out the side door. I couldn't process what my ears just heard. My dad? My perfect dad? My hero? He slept with a black woman. I fell to my knees and began crying all over again. This couldn't be true. How could I have not known this my whole life? How could I have been so blind? How did I not know who my father really was? I was sick to my stomach. I was in disbelief. I lay there curled up in a ball, sobbing by myself. Nivea was right. Nivea knew, and I didn't.

~

I woke up on my living room floor and thought maybe it was all a bad dream. I was hoping I was right. I checked my phone to see I missed several calls and text messages. My uncle Rodney had called me three times, and Nivea called me about seven times. I had texts from Niv, Uncle Rodney, and an unknown number. It was 12:22 am, and I was wondering if anyone would be awake right now. I went to get up and felt my stomach turning in knots. As I am running to the bathroom, I start vomiting everywhere. Shit! Sitting by this porcelain throne makes me wonder how many nights my mom spent here. I just want this all to be untrue.

I text Nivea, *"Hey, you up?"*

Ping! *"Yes, are you okay? I am sorry. Let's talk, please."*

I am not sure I can drive, so I text her back to come over. Within minutes, Nivea is banging on my front door. I managed to get up and open it for her. Nivea came in like a cannonball, hugging me and saying how sorry she was for dropping this bomb of information on me. I couldn't cry anymore; I had cried so much earlier I had nothing left. We sat down on my front porch, and I explained to her that I was sorry for freaking out on her. I was out of line to act as if it was her fault my dad was a cheater. I told her that my mom confirmed it, and I was still trying to digest the fact that I had a black sister. I couldn't even fix my mouth to say those words. It was awful. It was disgusting. The more I thought about it, the more I wanted to throw up again. I crossed my legs and sat back in the huge fluffy chair in the corner with Niv sitting across from me in a similar chair. It was dark, and I could hear bugs fluttering about and dying on the lights hung around neighbors' homes.

Niv broke the silence, "Kayla, I know you probably don't want to hear this, but honestly, I think you should reach out to Tiffany. I found her on Facebook. She's a highly successful woman. She's older than you by a few years, so your mom and dad were newly married and had no kids at the time. She grew up in Chicago and probably never saw or met your dad. Maybe she deserves to know about him or her siblings. She is innocent in all this. It's not like she asked to be born. I really think you should give her a chance."

I couldn't believe my best friend was trying to get me to be friends with my dead father's love child. The pain and anguish I feel right now is unbearable. I have no desire to meet her.

"Niv, I don't think you understand. I don't want anything to do with her. Even if she was innocent in it, she's a nigger!"

Nivea stood up and walked over to me, looking down at my crossed legs, "You know what, Kayla? I hate that word, and I have always hated that your family is racist. What did black people ever do to you? Why do you hate them so much? I hope one day you realize all that hate you have for her is also hate for your precious father because she has his blood, and clearly, he liked her momma!" She walked off and slammed my door so hard I heard a picture fall off the wall. I took a deep breath and rubbed my face as hard as I could with my sweaty hands. I am going to have to figure this out, but right now, I needed to get something in my stomach. I grabbed my keys and my purse and left for Whataburger.

22

Nivea

"Miranda, I found some old photos of you as a baby. Come see." Miranda headed over to sit by me and look through her grandmother's old photo album. There was so much stuff in this house to go through, and I was waiting for a treasure to pop up. I was hoping all old people had hidden treasure, and when they died, someone would find it and never have to work again. So far, there was no treasure in old Mrs. Levitt's house. I kept digging through all the boxes we found in the attic and came across some more newspaper clippings. It seems Mrs. Levitt had a thing for collecting current events. I started looking at each title, and they were all for her son winning championships in football. Apparently, Miranda's uncle was a big deal back in the day. The papers covered his games and named him most likely to make it in the NFL.

"Hey Randa, did your uncle ever play in the NFL? Did he make it?" Miranda looked in my direction, and I handed her the articles. "Oh my gosh, Uncle Aaron when he was a star. This is crazy because my uncle Aaron never played football after high school. As a matter of fact, he is bald and has a huge beer belly." She started cracking up. "Could you imagine if he made it? He probably stood a chance from what I've heard, but he was too busy chasing after my aunt Toni. They married, and he never looked back at football again." I don't remember him, and I am guessing he doesn't live around here. However, I was surprised he chose a girl over a career with millions. Why not marry the girl and play football?

I continued digging through my boxes until Miranda's mom arrived and said, "Let's call it a day." My favorite part of our afternoon.

Miranda, her mom, and I walked into Francesca's for dinner. Francesca's has the best Italian food around. It smells amazing in here, and the garlic bread is to die for. They treat you to their signature wine trio and allow you to taste test the new flavors of wine they offer. I voted for a bottle of the strawberry sangria, and thankfully, the table agreed. After a few glasses and a lovely meal of fettuccine alfredo, I was ready to head to the bar. I asked Miranda and Jen if they wanted to tag along. Miranda agreed, and Jen said she needed to get some sleep but for us to have a drink for her. I never have a problem drinking for anyone else. I ordered us an Uber and we waited outside while Jen took off in her Prius.

"Miranda, can I ask you a personal question?" I think the wine gave me confidence. I was feeling extra bold.

"Yea, sure anything" I was ready like a waiting volcano.

"Are you racist?" Miranda looked stunned. She started laughing hysterically at my question.

"Wait, are you serious? Nivea, no, hahahaha, my ex-boyfriend is black, I've dated Hispanic men, Asian men, and all races in between." I had to pick my jaw up off the pavement.

"Miranda, I knew I liked you. I really did." Just then, our Uber pulled into the parking lot, and we hopped in the car.

∼

Since I chose not to open my shop on Wednesday after all the shenanigans with Kayla and her sister, I decided there was no way I could close on Thursday too. I had to come in and help my precious Mrs. Robins. She was going to be a breath of fresh air after the last couple of days. I was hoping she came alone and didn't bring Jessica. I needed a break from all of Kayla's drama. I went in the back and got her rinse ready for the shampoo bowl and brought out my rollers to set up by my station, and in she walks.

"Niv, honey, thank you for taking me. I was watching the news, and it's gonna rain, child. I need my hair extra tight and fluffy with lots of spray." I love this woman. She is always worried about her looks. Even in her eighties, the lady wants to be stunning. You gotta give her credit for not letting herself go.

"Mrs. Robins, you know I got you. Come here and have a seat."

After washing her silver curls and applying the rinse to make her color flow and dissipate any yellowing, I brought her over to my station to start rolling her hair. Mrs. Robins asked me how I was doing and what has been going on with me. This was normal conversation for a stylist and her client, but Mrs. Robins was like a grandmother to me, and I couldn't help but feel comfortable telling her all about Kayla. I needed someone to talk to, and an elderly lady seemed the perfect fit because she could give me the best advice. Older people were full of wisdom. I felt confident that Mrs. Robins wouldn't judge any of the story and look at Kay or her dad, God rest his soul, any differently.

"Well, you see, my life has been crazy, and I had to take some time off this week because of it. My best friend, you remember Kayla, right?" She nodded and laughed. Of course she knew Kayla because her mom was the talk of the town, and there wasn't a resident in Lutz that didn't know Slim or her poor daughter that had to care for her. "Well, the thing is, Mrs. Robins, I found out that Kayla's dad had an affair before she was born and had a love child with a black woman named Seven. I felt the information was too important not to share, and therefore, I told Kayla. She didn't take the news all that well, and things got a little crazy. I think she has calmed down now but still needs to come to terms with it all."

Mrs. Robins was silent, and this was unusual for her. I felt like I needed to keep talking to fill the air with words because it was almost uncomfortable. I started to think I made a mistake sharing this story with Mrs. Robins, and then she broke the silence with two words, "I know." I stared at her in my mirror, and she looked me right in the eye as we stared in silence. My jaw was wide open, and I was so confused my face was giving it all away. She cleared her throat and spoke really slow, "Nivea, sweetheart, don't go drudging up the past, especially someone else's. This town has secrets, and some secrets are best kept hidden. Kayla's father was a good man, but when her momma found out about his affair, she and her brothers made sure he paid for it. The sheriff isn't someone you want to mess with, Nivea dear. I don't want anything to happen to you. Do me a favor and stay out of that family's affairs."

This news was shocking. I wanted to ask Mrs. Robins a million questions, but I knew she was done talking. She wanted me to let it go and move on. I couldn't believe she said Kayla's mom and uncles made sure he paid for it. What did that mean? I decided I'll end this conversation here in my shop, but my investigation is just starting.

23

Kayla

I don't want to get out of bed today. I got nothing done yesterday because I am still trying to process all the information dumped on me about my father. Yesterday, I stayed in my bed and slept on and off due to stress and exhaustion. I move out in two days, and I have so much to do. I literally feel like it's never going to get done. My phone started ringing, and I felt around my bed looking for it as the buzzing was vibrating my whole body. The screen displayed the name *Uncle Rodney*. I didn't want to answer because I assumed it had something to do with my mom, and that was the last thing I wanted to deal with. I slid the green line over to answer the phone.

"Hello."

"Kay, you home?" I sighed because I knew where this was going; my mom was probably found somewhere drunk, and he needed to bring her to me. I think I just found all the motivation I needed to pack my stuff and move out.

"Yea, I'm here."

"Stay put. I'm on my way over." With those words, the line went dead, and I lay back on my bed, grabbed my pillow, shoved my face in it, and screamed as loud as I could. My life was falling apart, and I couldn't pick up the pieces fast enough. I got myself dressed to be somewhat decent for my uncle's uninvited arrival and then walked out to sit on the porch. It's extremely hot already and humid. It feels like rain is in the air. Normally, I hate the rain here in Florida, but today, I kind of welcome the glooming dark skies since it's fitting for my life. Uncle Rodney pulled in his cop car and walked up to the porch dressed to the nine in his pristine sheriff uniform. I sat there staring out the window, looking for my mom. I didn't see her in the car or anywhere for that matter. Uncle Rodney walked on the porch and removed his sheriff's hat. At this point, I was nervous, and I jumped up from my seat and felt like I couldn't breathe.

"Is my mom okay? What's this about? What's going on?"

Uncle Rodney asked me to sit back down, and I could feel the tears welling up in my eyes.

"Your mom is fine. She told me you found out about your daddy's affair, and I wanted to make sure you don't go reaching out to this girl. Your daddy made a big mistake, but my sister can't take no more pain, ya hear? You need to leave this whole thing alone. No need to dig up old information and go searching around for things that are better left alone. Now I'm warning you, Kay, if I find out you been doing more digging, you gonna be sorry. Now that's not a threat, young lady; it's a promise. Now I gotta get back out on the road, but I need to know you understand. You get what I'm saying?"

I didn't know how to take this deep, authoritative voice he was projecting. Uncle Rodney has never spoken to me like this before. I just simply replied with a "Yes, I understand."

"Good. Take care now." I guess this is why he's been calling, and I had all those missed calls a couple of days ago. Now I wish I would've just called him back. It felt like I was in trouble when I was the one who got hurt here. Why is he worried about my mom? Slim already knew, and she's been a drunk since he died. What about me? What about, *hey Kay, so sorry you found out your perfect vision of dad is now tarnished. Sorry we never told you your dad was a nigger lover. How you feeling? You okay?* No, it's always about Slim and how she is and what she needs. Why does he protect her like that? Jerimiah never protected me like that, and I doubt he ever would. They have a weird relationship, and I am twenty-three years old. I can do or investigate whatever I want. Who does he think he is telling me I can't learn more about my dad. I went back into the house where the AC was blasting and grabbed my phone. It was much cooler in here, and I needed the cool air to think straight. I remember Nivea telling me my sister was on Facebook. I opened the app and started typing in her name, Tiffany Gray, and several came up. I had to think about what Niv told me, and my mind was a blur like I blocked it out. I refused to text her and ask her, so I decided I would figure it out myself. Her mom's name was Seven. How many Sevens could possibly be out there? I typed in the name Seven and hit search. To my surprise, lots of people in the world name their kid after a number. I looked for one in Chicago with brown skin. I clicked on profile after profile until boom. There she was, Seven Moore Lyons of Chicago, Illinois. I clicked on her photos and began looking at all the ones that were not private. I started to cry as I scrolled through the pictures. Seven was beautiful, she wasn't ghetto, but in fact, she was very well put together. Way more than Slim. She had several pictures of her and Tiffany together. Tiffany's graduation from high school and college. Her in a pair of scrubs, standing with who I assume is her stepdad. They have a beautiful family. They look happy, and I see so much love in these photos. They take vacations to extravagant places. They spend a lot of time together, something my family lacks—love! We don't spend holidays around a big table full of family and friends. We don't even talk to each other half time. Tiffany, my sister, is a doctor. A well-established smart doctor! Seven tagged her in a photo of the two of them standing on a beach in Hawaii. The photo was picture perfect. My sister has a noticeably light complexion, and her mom is more of a caramel. I clicked on Tiffany's name in the photo, and it took me to her page. It seemed her page was not private. She had nothing to hide. Photos of her during graduation and med school. All her friends wearing their sweatshirts splattered with their University across the front. Everyone was smiling and happy. They look successful and established like everything just fell into place for them. I scrolled through each one of Tiffany's photos and watched her life like a movie. I couldn't help but feel overwhelmed with emotion. Tears ran down my cheeks like a waterfall. This girl was innocent. Nivea was right. She was just living her life to the fullest, and I was over here working at the same diner I always have, cleaning up my mom's puke every night. I wonder what she would think of me. I wonder if she would hate me for being white or for having her real dad live with me. I wonder what she acts like or talks like or if she knows about me. What if she never knew she had a biological father living in Florida who was murdered? What if her mom never told her? Oh my gosh, I don't know what to do. A huge part of me is dying to send her a message, and another part of me is scared shitless. I just have to do it. I clicked on *message*, and it opened the Messenger app on my phone. The black line just sitting there flashing, waiting for the letters it will reveal at my fingers' request. I stared at the screen, thinking, *how do I start this? Hi, I am your sister, um… your white sister.* Oh my… my thoughts were interrupted by my mother strolling through the side door. I quickly turned my phone off and put it on the couch next to me. She didn't look drunk, which was surprising to me.

"Did your uncle Rodney come by here and talk to you?" She lit her cigarette on the stove as per usual and inhaled a huge puff of smoke she blew out through her nostrils.

"Yea, don't worry, I won't go stirring up trouble for you." I was hoping this would end the conversation because I had nothing more to say to her, especially since I was lying through my teeth. I was hoping she didn't notice the shakiness in my voice.

"Kayla, I'm sorry you had to find out like this and that it hurt you. I never wanted you to think your father was anything less than a good man. I miss the hell out of him, and I'm sorry I haven't always been there for you during these past few years."

Wow, she really just downplayed her role. In the past "few" years. Who is she kidding? More like the past thirteen years. However, she apologized, and I have never heard my mother say sorry for being so terrible over these past "few years" I will take it.

"I got to lay down; I have a headache. I know you're moving out; you don't have to hide it anymore." I wasn't sure how she knew this, but that was the end of the conversation because she headed to her room. I assume the headache is her body going through withdrawal from no alcohol. I wonder what life would be like if she was sober all the time. Why now would she sober up? I felt guilty for lying, but I also didn't want to hurt her or send her on a spiral down bad memory lane. No need to fight with her; the woman is scarred, and beyond repair. I don't want to be the reason she lets go for good.

~

I went out to purchase more boxes for moving, and while out, I ran into Josh. I couldn't believe it! There he was, standing right in front of me at the UPS store. I wasn't sure how to act or what to say, or if I should leave or hide. I didn't know what to do. I was frozen and started sweating from my brow and my hands. My heart was racing, and I felt like my mouth was so dry I could use my tongue for sandpaper. I watched him insert his card to pay for a package he was shipping, and his arms looked bigger than I remembered. I could see muscles that I never noticed before. His watch looked expensive, and his hands were well-manicured like always. He brushed his fingers through his long hair on top of his head and down the bare part of his neck, and I heard him laugh. I wasn't sure what the clerk said or what had happened because I was so caught off guard just staring at this man, I missed any part of the conversation relevant to him acting embarrassed. I saw him slip his card in again and realized the clerk was advising him it declined. I felt this horrible pain in my gut, and I knew I had to do something. I didn't want Josh to feel embarrassed. I felt obligated to save him.

"Hey, there you are! I was looking for you in the store. Oh no, not this card. I moved the money to the other account. Here you go, madam, I see the total is $40 dollars correct? I have cash. Also, I will need a second transaction. I will need to purchase some moving boxes, the XL ones you carry, please. I need five."

The look on his face was astonishment, but I was glad I was there to help. We walked out together.

"Hey, Kay, listen…"

I interrupted him, "Josh, don't I know what you're gonna say, and it's okay; that's what friends are for." I smiled up at his tall physique, taking in the differences of his face and hair in the last year that we have been broken up. He is still beautiful in every way. Still a perfect smile and clear complexion with no facial ever. The boy couldn't grow a beard if he tried. It was almost comical what a babyface he had.

"Kay, I will pay you back. It's not your problem, I have money, I just... I don't know what happened... I..."

"Josh, seriously, it's okay; no need to defend your finances to this girl, I promise. I am just happy to see you. I am really glad you reached out to me on Facebook and sent that message. It meant a lot. Consider this my thank you."

He took a deep breath and exhaled it slowly but loud.

"Yea, well, I got to get going. Thank you then, for paying for that. I'll see you around, Kay." He walked off to the parking lot, and his smell lingered behind. It was a familiar fragrance, and I wanted to keep it. Keep this moment I wanted to hug him and ask him about Jessica and what happened to him and tell him how sorry I was I never noticed. I felt that pang in the pit of my stomach like I was a chaser and he did not want to be chased. Clearly, I was more excited to see him. He must be dealing with a lot of demons right now. I wish he would talk to me because you know what, Josh? Me too, me too.

24

Tiffany

It's been four days since Daniel and I went out, and we have been inseparable. I cannot believe I waited so long to reel him in. He is the perfect gentleman, and I am incredibly comfortable around him. I cannot get him off my mind ever. This man is everything I could ever want in a human. I checked my Apple watch more than my pager these days just to see if he texted me. By six pm, I was doing my rounds, checking on patients, when my watch pinged, and I looked to see if it was Daniel. It was my mom.

"Tiffany, this is urgent. I need you to call me as soon as you are free."

I hit the auto-reply on the watch *"OK"* and finished my rounds. I wasn't sure what could be so urgent. There was really nothing ever going on in her life. I would know if there was;

we tell each other everything. I was free around nine pm and grabbed my phone from my locker to call mom back.

"Hello." She always answers with the same hello like she doesn't know who is calling her.

"Mom, hey, I don't have a lot of time. What's going on?" She was starting to cry, and I could hear it in her voice she was doing her best to hide it. "Mom, are you okay?"

As she was trying to get herself together, the words fell off her tongue, "Your father had a heart attack, Tiffany. He is at Northwestern Memorial, and I am all but losing my mind. These doctors rushed him into surgery, and I haven't heard anything. They told me his aortas were separating, and they found holes on his heart like a sponge, and oh my God, Tiffany, if I lose him, oh my…"

She was crying loudly now, and I knew it was serious. I had to get off the phone and get to the hospital. I let my supervisor know what was going on, and then I texted Daniel. He worked at Northwestern Memorial, and I knew he could give me inside information. I was on my way to the north side when I got a reply from Daniel letting me know my father was in critical condition and they didn't know if he would make it through surgery. He advised me in medical terms that my father might be a vegetable. I could barely drive. I was crying and panicking, and my brain normally works really well under pressure, but this was different; this was my dad. Damian Lyons was the best father figure ever.

He took my mom and me in when I was still in the womb. My real father was in my life when he could be, but he was married. My mother never kept this information from me. She allowed me to decide how close we were. I was happy that he came to pick me up and took me for ice-cream or attended my dance recitals on all his business trips to Chicago. He was such a fun guy, and he always made me laugh. He would bring me gifts and give my mom money for anything I needed. He was always polite to Damian and thanked him for doing such a great job raising his baby girl. My birth father, Tony, was an investment banker. He worked a lot and lived in Florida. I never asked him many questions about his life. I had Damian. Damian was there for everything. He didn't come and go. He lived with me. He taught me how to walk, talk, eat, hold a spoon, manage money, and do well in school. Damian was amazing and treated my mom like a queen. He taught me the way a woman should be treated. He never let me forget that mommy and I were important and deserved the best. He was at every parent-teacher conference and college visit. He came on field trips and took me shopping. Damian was a dad, and he was my dad. My real father died when I was just thirteen. I remember when my mom came to my room to tell me. I had just spent the weekend before with him. I couldn't believe it. Murdered? I still remember being shocked. I remember asking my mom to save me any newspaper articles she had pertaining to my fathers' death. I learned from those papers that I had a brother and sister. I couldn't believe my dad never told me about them. Jerimiah and Kayla! They were younger than me, and I wondered what they thought about me. It was a super cold rainy day when my mom sat me down and explained to me that he was married. He had a wife and a family and couldn't tell anyone about me. I was a secret. I figured back then it was just because I was the product of an affair but learned later that it had a lot to do with the color of my skin. This news kept me from reaching out to my siblings. I get enough racism in my face just walking down the street; I didn't need it from an estranged family. My mother always left it up to me to reach out to them and make a relationship, but I never felt the need. In fact, Damian was such a good father I didn't miss my dad all that much. I embraced Damian as my father and moved on. It's not like I saw my father all that much. My mother had several photos of us together when I was younger. I still have an entire album dedicated to our relationship, but I never visit it. It remains in my old bedroom at my parents' house. Before my father passed, Damian got his permission to adopt me. I gratefully accepted the news of the adoption and considered myself a Lyons. My mother thought it best to keep my father's last name as my middle name. There it was on my new birth certificate, Tiffany Gray Lyons. The news of Damian being in the hospital from cardiac arrest is excruciating compared to my birth father. Just because we share DNA doesn't make him my dad. We are just related. I have nothing but positive memories about him, but he kept me a secret because I was black. I'm not sure I can ever grasp that concept. Damian has never denied me!

~

I parked by the front entrance and ran inside. I already knew where I was going, I had interned here, and I was aware of the hospital's layout. I texted Daniel that I had arrived at the hospital and would be in the cardiology unit. When I got off the elevator, my mom was there on the floor, inconsolable. I couldn't get to her fast enough, and I told the doctor holding her I was her daughter and introduced myself. The doctor looked at me and apologized.

"Sorry for what?" It was as if I forgot how to speak doctor at that moment. When I realized what was going on, I lost it with my mom on the floor. I cannot remember how or when I ended up in an empty hospital bed, but I was in Daniel's arms when I came to.

"Hey, you. Can I get you anything?" I was beyond dreary and felt sick. I was hoping I just woke up from a bad dream, but I knew that wasn't the case. Daniel is here; I am in a hospital. It was real; it was very real. My father, Damian Lyons, didn't make it.

"Daniel, where is my mom?" He rubbed my back, put a finger to his lips to shush me, and pointed to the bed across the room. My mother was sleeping like a baby, tissues still in her hand. I couldn't believe this was happening. Damian was supposed to see me finish my residency. He still needed to walk me down the aisle and give me away. How could this have happened? I couldn't even accept it for the medical reasons. I was blaming everyone in the hospital and screaming at the doctors. Daniel said it was bad enough that they gave both me and my mom a sedative and put us in this room to sleep it off. The pain my patient's families go through is now very real. I just walked in their shoes. I just stood in that waiting room holding a grieving widow, my mother. I was that person who was always on the other side, the one who said, "I am sorry," not the other way around. Tears filled my eyes, and I leaned over on Daniel's chest and begged him to tell me it wasn't true. I knew it was; I just didn't want to be true, and a part of me thought that somehow, someway, Daniel could fix it. My legs were not stable enough to walk after the sedative, and Daniel recommended I stay put in the bed. He brought me some coffee and a bagel, but I couldn't eat. I felt like a part of me was gone forever, and I couldn't begin to comprehend my new life without my father. I needed him. Mom needed him. We needed him!

25

Jerimiah

The airport is extra busy with all the summer travelers making their planned vacations with their families. Lots of children crying and playing on electronics while Mom and Dad are busy making sure they didn't forget anything. I walked holding hands with Keith, rolling our suitcases behind us. This was it. I was going home, a shaking, scared man who also felt more confident than ever before. I was ready with every ounce of blood pumping through my veins to explode my truth. I wasn't sure how this would go down or what to expect, and the unknown was killing me. I briefed Keith on my family and everything we should expect when we get there. I explained there would be no loving embrace or, "Oh, J, we already knew." It would be a moment involved with lots of cursing, screaming, and the cherry on top, "You're dead to us, get out." The reaction would be cold, and I had to be ready. I was hoping that maybe my sister and I could rekindle our relationship and she would love me no matter what faults I had, but I also had to accept that I was asking for the winning lottery numbers with that kind of hope. I sat down at our gate next to Keith and stared out the window. Life was so beautiful here in SF, and I thought about how different it was in Lutz. How people were so critical and judgmental and how they were stuck in the past, and no one accepted anything other than the Bible as a way of life. Growing up in that town was supposed to guarantee you were going to do all the right things in life. Anything off the perfect path was considered an outcast. I knew this was going to be the toughest thing I've ever done, but here I was, ready as ever.

There was a Starbucks in the airport, and I decided to get Keith and me a drink. As I was walking up to the counter, a little girl ran right in front of me and tripped over my foot. I bent down to help her up and apologized for not seeing her. Even though this was not my fault, I felt bad for the kiddo, who clearly wasn't listening to her mother. I saw the tears streaming down her face, and I smiled at her and told her it would all be okay. Her mother came over and apologized and told me she was having a rough day after nonstop flying. I didn't need any explanation; I was mesmerized by the little girl. She was beautiful even with her bump on her forehead and water eyes. She was the cutest thing, and I thought I couldn't wait to have kids. I am going to be a much better parent than my own mother. I will be the mother mine was prior to my father's passing. I was going to make sure my kids knew they were loved and accepted no matter who or what they decided to become in life. The thing about growing up with the Bible in your town is that everyone wanted to preach the right way of life, but oddly enough, they missed the big picture. Love the sinner, not the sin. Just as our Father loves us, we should love others. We have this right of passage to be like Jesus, who washed the feet of the poor and loved a woman who was an adulterous, yet they are quick to judge me. Everyone is quick to say what someone else is doing wrong but never do they look at their own life. I hope that when we leave Tampa, we will have created a peace among us, but I doubt that will be the case. Either way, I am fine saying goodbye to my family once and for all. I have made my mind up that I am gay, and I am not going to be anything other than gay. This is who I am, Jerimiah Gray, the man who fell in love with another man and no longer wants to hide it.

~

Once we were in the air, Keith fell asleep. I couldn't sleep if I wanted to because my mind was racing a million miles an hour about how this surprise visit would go down. I was glad we were staying in the city and not in Lutz. I sat there staring out the window, looking at the world, thinking how different things looked now that I was brave enough to own my true self with no regrets. I could see clearly. I thought about how much heartache had been put upon me with losing my father and my mother at the same time. My mother changed, and no longer was the brilliant loving super mom. She needed real help but never got it. My father was the glue that held the family together, and none of us picked up that role when he died. I was only six at the time, and taking on the role of the man of the house was asking quite a lot. Kayla never let go of losing our father. I can see the hurt in her eyes. She also has never been the same but likes to blame my mom for all of it. It's funny, you know; we came from the same parents with the same DNA, yet we are so different in our views and lifestyles. Kayla is always the good girl, doing what is right and working hard to please everyone. On the other hand, I don't care what the family thinks or how they feel; this is my life. Sometimes, I wish Kayla were more like me, but I am positive she wishes I were more like her. A yes man. Always willing to help out and be the protector of her and Mom. Maybe I should have, and maybe if I did choose that route, things would have been different for all of us, but this is who I am. I put my head on Keith's shoulder and took in his smell; he is everything I have ever wanted. He makes me feel safe and like I could literally move mountains. I love this man with everything in me. I couldn't imagine a world where I had to pretend to love a woman. I would rather die than be faced with a forced marriage and life. I closed my eyes and prayed that God would give me the words to say to my family to help them accept me. Being up here in the sky, I felt close to God, and I feel like he heard my cry for help.

26

Kayla

I t is Saturday morning, and finally, I am moving out of this house. I can't believe I am taking this giant step toward adulthood. I have everything packed up and ready to go when the movers get here. I am thrilled to finally be leaving all this drama. It's weird how now that I am moving out, I am looking at this house differently than before. I see it now for all of its hate and hard times. There is no love in these rooms or walls. There are no happy memories of sitting at the table having a holiday dinner. No swing set rotting in the backyard from the excessive heat that contains happy times of children playing together. This is not a home. It is a vault of terrible nightmares, and I wish I could burn it down. As I walked into the kitchen to make something to eat, I saw my mother sitting on the couch. The ugly floral print furniture that has never been replaced. She looked thinner than normal, and of course, she was smoking a cigarette. She turned to look at me, and I asked her if she was hungry. I wasn't sure if she was drunk or hungover, but either way, I didn't care because I was moving out and moving on. I was no longer her muse.

"No, I am not hungry." I wasn't surprised by her response because she barely ate. I got myself some cereal and sat down adjacent to her on the chair with the matching hideous floral print. "Kay, I need to talk to you." I was worried when I heard these words. The last thing I wanted was for her to beg me to stay. Please don't beg me to stay. I was staring at her so hard I could feel my eyes bulging, begging her not to say those words. *Let me go*, I said over and over in my head, *just let me go, Mom, please*. "This is going to be hard to say, and I want you to know I am sorry for the pain this will cause you." Pain? Does she know how badly my pain really is? What does she know about pain? I was getting irritated fast. I already found out my father had an affair with a black woman, and I have a half-sister who is a successful doctor and lives in Chicago. She had a wonderful upbringing while I sat here and took care of my alcoholic for a mother. Sure, Mom, lay it on me; what other pain can you cause? It's like adding salt to a wound, and she is a pro at this. "This story is going to make you look at people differently, and I am ready to face that. I know I haven't been an exceptionally good mother, but maybe you will finally understand why." She lit up another cigarette and began to cry. I was literally rolling my eyes. I can't wait to hear her excuse for why she was a bad mom. We have been down this road so many times I can recite it like it's my job.

"I'm listening, Mom." I tried not to let the frustration in my voice come through, but it did anyway. My tone was all but polite. Here we go. I put my cereal down next to me on the end table and sat back in the chair. I pulled my legs up to my chest and pulled my big t-shirt over my legs, placing my chin on my knees. I waited patiently while she inhaled and exhaled on her smoke.

"When your father and I first got married, we lived in Tampa, as you know. We had a great life. Tony was remarkably successful at the bank, and his career was taking off. He started traveling quite a lot, and that's when he got Seven pregnant. She worked for a bank, and they met up at a convention, or so that's what your father told me. I didn't find out right away. I had already given birth to you and your brother by the time I found out. The girl, Tiffany, she was older than you. I only figured out something was going on because he started spending a lot of time in Chicago. He was no longer wanting to travel for work to other places even if it paid more. At one point, he was offered a promotion and turned it down because there would be no more trips to Chicago. I couldn't understand it, so I figured he must be cheating and started digging. Of course, I asked your uncle Rodney to assist because he is a cop after all, and I knew he was a good detective. He wasn't the sheriff at the time, but as a seasoned office who was now a detective, he was my best chance at solving this puzzle. I found receipts for ice cream, I found recital tickets, I found the name Seven in his cellphone. This was the name and number he always used while in Chicago. I figured it out, and when I finally came to him with all the facts, he no longer denied it. He told me everything. He told me how he slept with Seven early on in our marriage and how she became pregnant. He told me that he needed to be there for his daughter and take responsibility. He told me he wanted to tell me sooner, but he knew I hated black people and was a racist bitch. He actually called me that, Kayla. Like I did something wrong when he was the one who cheated. He had the audacity to act as if my understanding of how disgusting niggers were was a fake reality. I couldn't even fathom that he came home and slept with me after sleeping with this black whore. I felt dirty! I felt like I could never get clean after that. I couldn't stop thinking about it. I never thought Tony would do this to me, never. I could have forgiven him for sleeping around, but with a black woman, Kayla, that was unforgivable. He had hidden his affair and this love child for years. Anyways, one night, I was hurting so bad I left the house and told Rodney everything. Your uncle Rodney and I decided right then and there your dad needed to pay for what he had done to me and you kids. The weekend was approaching, and Rodney told me we should go to dinner and he would take care of the rest. I would have an alibi, and he could cover the tracks. I was over your father at that point. I didn't love him anymore, and I wanted him dead. I hated him. He betrayed me. Rodney was a detective; he knew how to cover his tracks and make the crime scene look like a murder with no evidence. That night, I got ready and pretended to like your father while we went out, and then I let Rodney and Uncle Ben have their way with him. His murder was not solved because Rodney was the lead detective, and he knew he did it. I never told anyone. I've been carrying around this guilt for the last almost fourteen years. I turned to alcohol to deal with all the details of the murder. I got shitfaced drunk every night to cope with this life I had been dealt. I was now a single mom with two kids to raise, and I was responsible for their father's death. There were so many people asking questions and giving condolences. The thing is, I hated your father, but when he was gone, and I was left to take care of everything, it broke me. The stupid bitch Seven got money from his death, not just me. It took all I had not to kill her too. I was pissed. I thought when he was gone, I would have enough money to live a good life. Unfortunately, he had added his daughter to his benefits and life insurance. Kayla, please try to understand. I had to do what I had to do. Your father deserved it."

I sat there staring at her with tears running down my face, and I couldn't breathe. I couldn't think. My mother just confessed to me that she had my father killed. All this time, she knew I had a sister, she knew who killed my father, and here I was living in the house with a murderer, and her brother was helping raise us, the man who pulled the trigger. I couldn't believe this was happening. I started screaming. I was crying so hard I felt like I was about to pass out.

"How could you? HOW COULD YOU?" I screamed at her repeatedly. I felt sick to my stomach. I had to report the news. I had to tell someone. Who would believe me? Who do I call? How do I… How do I even start the story? How… Oh my gosh, this is not happening. I stood up and started pacing the floor back and forth. "YOU KNEW, YOU FUCKING KNEW YOU'RE A MURDERER." Just then, I heard the door slam, and I saw Jerimiah walk in with this guy I've never seen before. I couldn't deal with this. I ran to my brother screaming and crying, "Oh, J, I am so glad you are here." I hugged him so tight! I felt responsible for my baby brother. His shortcomings and our terrible mother. I didn't even care about his friend right now. I was so focused on my emotional state and this bomb that was dropped on me. Slim stayed in her seat with tears still streaming down her face as she smoked her life away.

"What is going on? Are you okay?" I lifted my head from J's chest, and I could barely say the words out loud.

"Uncle Rodney was the one who killed Dad. Mom made him do it; she murdered our father." I couldn't stand up anymore, and J helped me to the bar, where I sat down and tried to get a hold of myself.

"WHAT?" J walked over to Slim. "Is this true? Mom, tell me this isn't true."

Slim sat back on the couch and looked up at Jerimiah, her baby boy, who she doted on so much and loved more than anything.

"It's true, J, it's all true." She said, then she stood up and walked to the door. "Don't worry. I'm turning myself in today. I have suffered enough keeping this a secret, and now that you are both grown and moving on in your lives, there is no reason for me to hide the pain." I couldn't believe it. Just like that, she was going to turn her and her beloved Rodney and Ben into the authorities. I was in a nightmare, and I felt like I needed to wake up immediately.

I didn't say a word, but Jerimiah did. He took center stage to add gas to the fire, "I want to get my secret out too. I'm gay! This is Keith, my boyfriend, and I lied about going to school in San Fran. I moved there with Keith, and we live together. Whooo, that felt good." Jerimiah let out a huge sigh, smiled from ear to ear, and grabbed his lover's hand as if our mother didn't just tell us she killed our father. I felt like the crazy one in the family. Like, am I the only one who is recognizing what just happened?

Slim let go of the door, turned toward, and said, "I know J, I am happy for you." My jaw dropped, and I almost died right there. What was happening? My brother is gay, and my mom a murderer. I was out of words. Nothing could escape my lips. I had nothing left. Slim walked out the door and shut it hard behind her. I just sat there at the bar looking down at the old counter with all the scratched-up knife marks from everyone skipping the cutting board and just using the countertop instead. I stared at the tears that had fallen on the counter, making little puddles all over, and then I cracked. I was laughing so hard it took my breath away. I had tears pouring down my face and laughter spilling out of my mouth.

"Kayla, are you okay?" I didn't know at that point if I was crying from sadness and disappointment or from how hard I was laughing. I tried to calm myself down enough to speak, but it was hard to stop laughing.

"Yes, I am good, J. I am better than ever, as a matter of fact." J was still holding Keith's hand and walked with him to the other side of the bar to look at me. "Seriously, J, I am good. Dad died at the hands of Mom and Uncle Rodney, and I was left to pick up the pieces. She got drunk every day and puked on everything; she never took care of us or herself. You ignored us all, and now I know why; you were hiding behind a straight man. Dad had an affair, and it was with a black woman, and now we have a black sister. I mean, yea, I am good. I went from thinking life couldn't get any worse to this hellacious shit." I began cracking up again. "This was the icing on the cake. I can finally put it all to rest and…"

"WAIT, Kayla, what do you mean we have a sister? Where? How did you find this out? How come no one told me?"

I forgot for a second that J was not privy to this information and had no idea we had a sibling in Chicago. I stopped laughing at that point because I had to get my T's crossed and I's dotted correctly now; my baby brother needed me.

"J, the reason Mommy had Daddy killed was because he had an affair with a woman named Seven. She was a black woman who was in the same line of work as Daddy was, and they met at a convention. The details don't matter; a baby came of it. Her name is Tiffany. She's twenty-eight and a doctor living in Chicago. I found her on Facebook. Daddy knew about her and supposedly took care of her, which is how Mom found out and then had Uncle Rodney kill him. It was all planned. I don't know if Tiffany or whatever knows about us, but now, we know about her."

J was silent and pulled his hand away from Keith to use both hands a force to rub his head. I watched him smiling bigger with each stroke of his hair.

"Kay, this is awesome. I have never been happier. What's her last name? How do I find her on Facebook? Is it Gray? Is it Tiffany Gray? Oh, shit, I have a sister."

I was kind of surprised my brother was so excited to have this long-lost estranged sister when I was his sister sitting right here in his face. I was always here. Did he forget? Did he hear the part about her being black? I couldn't think straight. I needed some time to myself. I decided to give him all the information he needed, and he could do what he wanted, but I was out of here. I grabbed my keys and my phone, and before he could stop me or ask me anything else, I slammed the door and ran for my car. I doubt he cared because he seemed way more interested in this Tiffany than he did me.

27

Tiffany

Things this past week have been hard. Trying to help my mom plan my father's funeral is the last thing any child wants to do. I had no choice but to be there for her. I had to try and be strong just as much as she did for me. From choosing the funeral home, flowers, cards, time, and casket, I was all but put off by choosing the tombstone and graveyard. I am glad I have Daniel by my side; he makes me feel like everything will be okay, and I have nothing to worry about. He has been super helpful with all the arrangements and sleeping over to keep me from being alone. I wish now that I told my dad I was dating Daniel. He knew him from my college days and always liked him, but now I feel like I was jipped. I had no father to walk me down the aisle and give me away. No father for Daniel to ask permission to marry me.

My birth father was murdered, and my adoptive father was now deceased due to heart complications. I felt an empty void in my stomach. I missed him; I missed him beyond words. My mom asked me if I could post the funeral information on Facebook. Many colleagues and other professors would want to give condolences as well as family members. I logged into my Facebook and saw that I had a new message. I rarely went on social media since I was constantly working and thought maybe it was an old message from Daniel. When I clicked on the message, I saw it was from a guy named Jerimiah Gray. I had no idea who this was, and I was thinking the name sounded familiar, but I kept repeating it in a whisper to myself. Jerimiah Gray, Jerimiah! Jerimiah! OH MY GOSH! It hit me that this was my brother from my birth father. What could he possibly want or message me about? I was stunned, just staring at my phone. For a minute, I had forgotten why I even went on Facebook. I was so preoccupied with this message. I decided that before I went down this road, I needed to post my father's funeral arrangements. I put up the details of Crosby Funeral Home with the address in downtown Chicago and the hours for viewing the body and attending the funeral. When I was finished, I went back to my messages and opened the one from Jerimiah.

"Hello, my name is Jerimiah, and I was recently informed that you are my sister. I would love to meet you, if that's okay with you, of course. I live in Cali, but right now, I'm in Florida. When I fly back home, I can change my flight to stop off in Chicago. Lmk if you're down to meet up. Hope to hear back soon. Take care!"

I wasn't sure why, but a big part of me really wanted to meet him. He sounded not only nice but also super genuine. After losing my father this past week and then knowing my birth father is already dead, I have nothing left but my mother. It would be nice to include my siblings in my life. I chose to write back and offer to come to him in Florida to meet both him and his, err, our sister. This will definitely take some getting used to. Now I what to reply with. It's an awkward yet rewarding and invigorating moment for me.

"Jerimiah, wow, I can't believe it's you. I have no idea how you found me or know about me, but I would love to meet up. I have some time off right now, which is truly unusual. If you tell me what part of Florida you are in, I am happy to take a trip to come meet you and just get away. Life has been pretty crazy here for me. Take down my cell and text me. I look forward to it. 224-214-2090 xoxo"

I need more than anything to just get away. Had this unknown brother of mine contacted me sooner, I probably would have responded much differently, but due to my current circumstances, I am all for this trip. Life is like that sometimes. You just never know, but it has a way with timing.

∼

I decided not to share this news with my mother as it may send her over the edge. She has had a rough time, and this might not be the moment to lay this on her. I did tell Daniel, though, and he thought it was a great idea. We discussed any and all ulterior motives that may be lurking in the dark, and then we went forward with let's go to Florida. I checked hotels in the Tampa area and booked one by the beach. I figured, when in Rome, right? I found two flights for super cheap, which I was pleasantly pleased to have done. I went shopping for all things beach and hot weather. I couldn't wait to get away. I needed a break, and even though I did not get a lot of bereavement time, I was going to take what little time I had and use it to my advantage. I was over crying nonstop and thinking about how different life would be. I work myself to death and never get any time to relax. This was my opportunity to go out and live a little. A beach vacation never sounded so good. I needed a place to take my mind off all the stress, and more than anything, I was secretly excited to meet my brother. I have been waiting a long time, twenty-eight years to be exact, to meet my siblings. I wonder what Kayla will be like. I wonder how close they are and if there will be room for another sister. I was nervous, but I was also excited. I am leaving the day after the funeral. I have lots of packing and shopping to do. Oh gosh, I should bring gifts. Ugh! I have no idea what they like, shoot. I have got to figure this out. I can't show up empty-handed. Maybe Daniel will have some good ideas.

28
Nivea

I needed to take a day and hit up the city pool. I ended up at the rec center lying poolside on a red and tan lounge chair. I put on the tanning oil I recently bought, and I loved the smell; it gave me happy thoughts. I considered ordering a drink at the bar, but my attention was caught by the news interruption. Channel 9 news had a breaking story. Suspects have been named in the murder of Tony Gray. Rodney Romano and Joanna Gray have been placed in police custody and are awaiting a hearing. I literally ran to the bar because now I NEEDED a drink. I couldn't believe it. Slim was the one who killed Kay's dad. All this time, none of us knew, and yet, the suspects were hiding in plain sight. Holy shit. That was kind of genius. A cop and his sister. I wonder who else was involved. Oh crap. It just hit me I was engulfed in the story for all the wrong reasons. I should call Kay. Make sure she is good. I hit her up, but it went to voicemail. She's probably embarrassed and depressed. I know I would be. Her mom, the town drunk/druggie, who walks the streets looking like she's barely eaten in weeks. I know Kay takes care of her, but it is embarrassing, and now to have your mom on the news for your father's murder. Yea, I'd escape and ignore my phone too. I ordered a margarita with a double shot of tequila. I was flabbergasted. I decided to text Jerimiah and see how he was doing.

"*J, you good? Lmk if you need anything.*"

Jerimiah immediately responded.

"*Hey Niv, I am great. I am in town. Let's meet up. I want you to meet someone.*"

Oh, I guess Jerimiah got himself a little sweet thang, and it must be serious if he's ready for everyone to meet them. I always thought Jerimiah was a little gay. Guess I was wrong. Unless the person is a guy, in which case I was right. I decided to invite him to the city pool.

"*Dude, I am at the rec center sittin' poolside with a Rita. Come thru.*"

I got back the simple, "*K, see you soon.*"

I suddenly realized nothing in that conversation went south. What did he mean he was great? Maybe he hasn't watched the news. I will let that sink in when he gets here. It seems to be broadcasting every five minutes across the screen. I wonder what type of reaction he will have. This should be interesting. I think I'll order another margarita. I don't want to disappoint with my own reactions. '

∽

The rec center is located directly in front of the beach. It is the best city pool in town. Everyone loves it. It has a bar with all the glorious alcohol you could ever want. You get beach views and a sandy beach walk into the pool. It's like being at the beach minus the sand everywhere. They offer cabanas and a dance floor with tables and some of the best food you can find in all of Lutz. The parking lot is always packed, but there is plenty of street parking. It's cheap to spend the day here, all of $5, and if you have a membership, you can use the rec center and the pool. I choose not to use the rec center because I don't have time to work out here or play basketball or whatever else people do in there. I saw Jerimiah walking in and stood up to wave so he could find me. There he was, looking just like I remembered, but with a hot-ass guy I've never seen before. Now I am praying I was wrong. I secretly crossed my fingers behind my back and tried to smile through my gritted teeth, quietly repeating, "Please, no, do not be gay, please, just be his friend." It always seems the hot ones turn gay, and what a waste for a single girl like me. They walk over and with the most excitement I have ever seen on Jerimiah. He proudly introduces me to his boyfriend, Keith.

"DAMMIT! Oh, whoops, I said that out loud. My bad. I meant, hi, I'm Nivea. Nice to meet you, Keith. Oh, damn, I wish you weren't gay; I'd eat you up."

Jerimiah started laughing and looked at his masterpiece of a man, "Sorry, girl, he's all mine."

We sat by the pool having drink after drink while Jerimiah filled me in on all the drama. He told me about his mom confessing and turning herself in and how he finally admitted to being gay and hitting up Tiffany. Jerimiah and I always got along because he was a lot like me. Clearly, he colors outside the lines. I never cared if someone was gay or straight or trans. I like people, and I don't see color. I've never been blinded by the color of their skin, just their ugliness. If you are rude, it does not matter to me; if you are orange, green, blue, or any color of the rainbow, I will fight you. I never understood why this town was so gung-ho on making everyone as white as possible and never letting anyone else in. It's like a cult where they make up who and what they believe a person is. I see culture. I see the food that represents who they are and how they were raised by their beliefs and backgrounds. I see their heritage and hard work. The color of their skin makes no difference. At the end of the day, we all bleed blue blood till it hits the air and turns red. We all have a heart and stomach and two eyes. I see people for who they are and not what shade they can tan. I never understood that. Especially hating a child who is innocent and never asked to be born. We all have our problems, but color should not be one of them. Look around you at the issues we face; is color really that fascinating that we need to make it a huge deal about everything? I can't. I have better things to do, like making money, running my own business, and building my empire. Let the colors we have be what we own. I say shine your rainbow and glow up because we only get one life to live, and I refuse to waste it on useless hate. I decided to ask Jerimiah about Kayla since I haven't heard from her. It's weird with everything going on that she hasn't kicked my door down, begging for a shoulder to cry on. Jerimiah informed me that since the day his mom poured out all her truths like a waterfall, he hasn't heard from his sister either. I found that to be even stranger. I decided to text her to make sure she was okay.

"Kay Kay, haaaay, girl. I am out at the rec center. Come by. J is here. You good? I saw the news. I am here for you if you need me. Luv ya."

Unfortunately, there was no response from her. I figured in her own time, she would get back to me. No need to rush her into talking. The girl did just find out her father was murdered at the hand of her mother and uncle. I really can't imagine how that must have been the icing on the cake to the long-lost sister she never knew about. I decided to give her some space and let her come around when she felt ready.

29

Jerimiah

My life has turned upside down so quickly, but in a way, I actually feel relieved. I always tried to brave my way through life as a straight man doing all the right things. This reality that my family was actually hiding more skeletons in the closet than a haunted house was proof that I am not all that messed up. I never needed to be afraid of who I was or what I loved. My dad, whom I was never close with and barely remember, clearly had issues keeping it in his pants. My uncle Rodney, the renowned sheriff, was nothing but a dirty cop who broke the law and condemned others for doing it. The funny thing is I always adored my mom, and even she came up empty-handed at acting like a saint. It was all her idea to have the man killed, hide our half-sister from us, and become a drunk. It is amazing that my whole life, I was hiding who I really was in fear of being rejected when everyone around me was hiding more. They walked past me and smiled and hugged me and threw out the "I love yous" and how proud they were of me all while knowing the reason I had no father was their fault. I had a sister I never knew because of them! The only thought that kept brewing in my mind was Kayla! I wonder what secret she was hiding. Little Miss Perfect must be keeping something to herself as well. I mean, she is a product of a disturbed family. I wish I knew what it was because it may help her to stop rejecting everyone else. She has really pointed her nose up like she owns the place and the world owes her a favor. When did being a good daughter ever come with a trophy? Never. You do things because you want to and because they represent who you are and what you stand for. Kayla is suffering, and I miss my sister. I do love her, but I am so content in my life right now, it has no room for hatred. I hope one day she will come around and learn to love and accept me for who I am. I hope she wants to meet Keith and Tiffany. I doubt those terms will come to pass, but one can be hopeful. I haven't decided if I will visit my mom. I feel like I need to go see her for closure. Give her the opportunity to admit her wrongs and accept mine. I want to hear her say that it is okay to be gay. That she loves me no matter what. She owes me that. Like, seriously, mom, you killed my father. You lied about it. You failed as a parent. She can't possibly think she earned the right to judge me. I don't hate her even though I want to a little bit because she was clearly selfish in her reasoning for murdering her husband. Obviously, she was not cut from the tough-ass cloth because the bitch cracked. She literally spiraled out of control, carrying around that baggage. I kind of wonder what she is thinking about now. No alcohol to relieve the pain or make her numb and knocked out. Every day, she has to face her demons head-on. Me sleeping with a man, well, I am not sure that compares to a killer. I am going to run it by Keith, but I think before we leave this God-forsaken town once and for all, I will swing by the county jail. Maybe, just maybe, I can be reminded of the mom I knew and not the Slim she became.

30

Kayla

The sun is shining ever so brightly in my room again. I haven't left this spot for days. I haven't unpacked a single item or had a single meal. I don't even care anymore. All my life, I have tried to do what is right and tried to be the good daughter, sister, and niece. I had no idea the people I was worried about pleasing were the same people responsible for my pain. They were the same people who killed my father and covered it up. They let me live wondering what happened and if the person was still walking around our town, seeing me grow up or shop in the local Piggly Wiggly. I was flabbergasted. How could I be nervous the killer was lurking around the beach or in my section eating at the Diner when all along the killer was living with me. How could I have been so blind to think my mom and my uncle loved me and would never do anything to hurt me. I have nothing to say to them. Not only am I embarrassed that when I step outside, everyone knows my mother and the sheriff killed my father, but it also hit national news. I can't even move away and hope to be discreet and start over. They ruined my life. They stole my father's life, took my childhood, made me believe they cared and wiped every tear I cried from my eyes and told me to be strong. They reminded me the case was never closed and we would somehow find the person who did this. Uncle Rodney was all too happy to step up to the plate and be my father figure. All this because my father had an affair. My father betrayed me too. The man I missed and cried for year after year slept with a black woman. He had another daughter. Not just me! I had a sister, and he never told me. He never alluded to the fact that he had a secret family or slipped up and said her name. He was a Bonafede liar. He was good at it. I felt like if he had lived, my life would have been better; my mom would have been better. She never would have drunk herself stupid every night, and J would have had a male figure to provide the right way of living. J would have never considered being gay. Now I hate him too. Everyone in this family was keeping secrets. They all had skeletons in the closet that did not creep out but jumped out at the same time. I guess the saying is true that when it rains, it pours. I can't stop crying, and yet I feel like no one deserves my tears. Josh wants nothing to do with me. I have no one who understands because Niv thinks this all is no big deal like with everything in life. She sways with the wind, whichever way it blows. Her lack of empathy makes me pissed at her too. Mr. H called to see how I was doing, but I think that was just to be polite because in the same message, he made sure to tell me I need to take some time off. He doesn't want me causing drama at the Diner. He thinks it's best if I stay home till things blow over. That was to be expected, I guess. Why would he want the biggest news story in the history of Lutz to be walking around his establishment and waiting on his loyal customers? That is the thing with this town. He would lose business. People would avoid it and tell him to fire me. No need. I decided to beat them to the punch and quit. I have no idea how I will pay for this apartment or what will happen to my mom's house. I feel like, again, it's all on me to figure it out. I am turning twenty-four years old, and I have nothing to be proud of or show for myself. A dead father, a murderous mother, a gay brother, no job, a half-black sister! How did this happen? My life was perfect till I was ten. I wish I could just pretend I never knew any of this. Just go back to the moments of being a little girl and loving my daddy as my hero. Now that is all gone. This sister of mine is a doctor. She's probably going to try and look down on me for not having a career, but pssshhh, she can't say anything because she's black. At least I got the right color from my parents. I can't look at my baby brother the same. I can't visit my mom in jail. I cannot get off this damn floor. I have no desire to live anymore. I feel hopeless, and now, with every tear falling from my cheek onto the gray carpet of this new apartment, I think, *how do I start over? How do I pick up the pieces and move on?* I grabbed my phone and saw I had several new messages. Niv invited me to the pool to chill with her and my brother. Who does she think she is? That is my brother. Why does she think it's okay to hang out with him? Ugh! J texted me and told me he invited Tiffany to town to come meet us. Was he crazy? She is the reason our father is dead, and our mother is in jail. Why can't he see that? She has ruined our lives. I have no desire to meet her. I couldn't care less if she were dead. I was going to have to break my lease and move. I couldn't stay here anymore. I had messages and missed calls from aunts and uncles. I had nothing to say to any of them. I didn't care anymore. I was going to make a list of things to do, and the list would be titled, *Goodbye, Kayla!* I would start with changing my number and my name. The first stop would be AT&T, and the second stop Lutz County Courthouse. I was going to disappear. No one was going to know who I was or where I was from. I have never left the country, but I decided that shouldn't be that hard since I also never lived with a murderer either till now. What was a flight to a foreign place in comparison to living with a killer?

31

Tiffany

My father's funeral was beautiful. We had over 500 people attend. My father was very well known for all his work with the University. The flowers were all white roses, and we made sure they covered the entire place. The choir sang and wore the most elegant white robes. It was a celebration of his life and his journey to becoming a renowned professor and all his accomplishments. My mother and I both spoke at the end, thanking everyone for attending and loving him as much as we did. He really was a special man. A vibrant old soul who anyone could get along with. We chose a light gray and white casket to match the roses and put him in a gray pinstriped suit. My daddy did love his suits. He was always shopping Steve Harvey's line and picking the most extravagant looks. Everyone knew him at the University for his ties. He always made a statement. We honored him, and he would have been proud of what Mama and I put together during all of our sorrow. It's not easy saying goodbye, but this felt more like see you soon. At the burial in the graveyard, we had the pastor read his favorite verse, a passage from Proverbs 17 verse 17, *"A friend loves at all times, and a brother is born for a time of adversity."* My father was a beautiful mentor to so many students. He loved his profession and took his work seriously. I feel honored to have had him in my life as long as I did. When he was placed slowly in the ground, we all let go of the balloons we were holding. All white and filled inside with different messages to be sent to Heaven. I looked up to the sky as the clouds slowly passed and the wind took hold of the balloons and smiled. I knew he was watching because I could feel his presence. Afterward, Mama and I went for a walk and talked, sharing memories, and laughing and crying. We showed up later to the gathering at a hall we rented and tried to eat the expensive food provided, but our sadness was too strong for hunger. We had a grand night just listening to people talk about Daddy and how much he inspired them and what a great friend he was all the while drinking away my tears. That night I slept like a rock. I was exhausted from the long day of preparation to the long starvation and too much alcohol.

∿

Daniel and I are all packed up and ready to hop our flight from Chicago O'Hare to Tampa Bay. I felt my nerves getting the best of me, and on the way to the airport, I almost threw up. This was strange to meet someone you share DNA with but have never seen or met in real life. It had me thinking, is DNA what makes a family? My adopted father was everything I could ever want in a dad, yet we shared no DNA. This kid, Jerimiah, he lived in a different world. After viewing his Facebook pictures and his interests, I noticed how much we did not have in common. He grew up with a mom who was an alcoholic, a home that looked like it was run down, and barely any friends. He was obviously gay and did not feel accepted. His page was somewhat depressing. I was not sure how we would fit together in making a connection, if any. I grabbed Daniel's hand and smiled at him. At least he was coming with me. I felt like there was no way I could do this alone. I just hoped my mom would be okay. I was worried about leaving her but also felt like I had to do this. I asked her to come, but she said I should meet my siblings on my own. I was praying they accepted me. You never know when you feel like the outcast. They had their mom and their dad, and then I was the product of an affair. Not sure that I am what the family would call a great addition. I am just hoping that Kayla and I can become close. I would love to have a sister, just do girly things, and hang out, talk about life and boys. I never had that except with my mom. It's going to be nice to have a little sister to kick it with. I heard the announcement for our flight and realized this was it; I was really doing this. Here we go, I thought as I boarded the plane. Here we go!

32

Slim

I haven't been sober in years, and being in here, in this 8x8 cell, has given me sobriety. Now, I am forced to face my demons and not drink them away. I've made my mistakes, and I now have to own up to them. I must face the fact that my husband's blood is on my hands. My brother is in jail because of me. I not only ruined my life, but now I also ruined his. He lost his career as a police officer, and his wife has filed for divorce. His children will not have their daddy to grow up loving and looking up to as a hero cop but rather a man who killed their uncle. I guess we all make choices we have to live with. That night when I went out with my Tony, I thought about how much I loved him and how we grew up together. I could not figure out when the connection was lost. When did he fall out of love with me enough to sleep with another woman? I felt betrayed. I had to wake up every day and play with our two children and clean our house and cook dinner all the while he was playing house with another woman. A secret love affair. An affair that equaled a baby. Not just a baby but a mixed child. We were never raised to talk to niggers. In our time growing up, they were considered less than us. We did not associate with blacks, and they did not associate with us. How did we go from such a beautiful love story to such a hellacious ending? It's strange how you think this kind of drama will never come to find you or your family. You think how someone else is crazy for what they did. I was that person too. I felt that there was no way I could kill someone or be responsible for having someone killed.

Tony and I had a beautiful marriage; we never argued or mistreated each other. He was my high school sweetheart, for crying out loud. I loved that man with every being inside me. Tony was more than just my husband, more than just a father to our beloved babies, but also my best friend. My only friend. He never lied to me, or so I thought until this happened. Tony and I were just two young kids who fell in love and wanted to live happily ever after with each other. The thing is, our families were close, and we attended all the dances together. We spent every holiday together, and I was there front and center cheering him on at every football game. We were inseparable. That was my lifeline.

When I fell pregnant the first time with Kayla, I thought about how wonderful it was to share with him our first child.

A girl! I knew Tony would be the best father ever, and this would be his little princess. We had a maternity shoot done, and I just felt like the world was all but gone and Tony and I were the only ones left. It was magical. A memory for the baby book that showed how much Mommy and Daddy loved their baby girl. When I gave birth to Kayla, he was right there holding my hand and pushing my sweaty hair off my forehead to give me a kiss. He was in awe of her, and I was in awe of them both. He picked her name. He said he loved K names and wanted to have a little girl with a beautiful K name. When he held her, he just stared like she was the most precious thing in life. He looked up at me and smiled in my dim hospital room. "Kayla," he whispered. "Kayla," I repeated, and that was her name. I knew they would have that bond that people dream of, and she was born to be a daddy's girl. I had no idea that at the time, Tony had already had his first kid; he had already experienced this moment with another woman. He had a baby girl, and this was his second time around. I was there draped in a hospital gown doped up on pain meds, thinking we just shared the birth of our first child. The one thing a girl dreamed about. The perfect family. I was wrong. I was alone in my excitement and hope for another child. Tony was already a father, and we didn't share anything special that day. It hurt my soul to find out he had a kid without my knowledge. He kept her a secret. He cheated.

I fell pregnant two years later and found out it was a boy. I was ecstatic, and Tony was as well. We both couldn't wait to decorate the baby's room and prep little Kayla for the big sister role. We ate ice cream that day after we found out it was a boy. I remember thinking, *how perfect, we have a girl and a boy; life was complete.* I found myself in pure harmony with Tony and our little family. All these pictures of us together like we were the model family. I was proud of my husband for how hard he worked in the finance world, and I thought I owed it to him to be the best wife. I stayed home to care for our kids. Jerimiah took to me like a natural momma's boy. He was my little ride or die. My kids were amazing. My life was amazing. I was never stressed about money. I never worried about much because Tony was a provider. A good one at that. He always made sure we were good. I just wanted him home more. I was struggling to survive being a mother alone. I had postpartum depression, and Tony was becoming more successful while I was becoming more unattractive. I was constantly changing diapers, cleaning, doing laundry, and the works. This did not include how much I was pumping and breastfeeding, along with never getting a shower. I felt like I was the ugliest wife, and I felt hopeless to ever be myself again. Every time Tony came home, though, he assured me I was gorgeous. He brought me flowers and gifts. He told me he missed me and loved me more than life. He played with our children and gave me a much-needed break to clean myself up. He failed to mention it was all a lie. He was really with his first daughter Tiffany. His precious Tiffany, whom he kept a secret from all of us. He liked playing house with two families, and I had no idea. I was so preoccupied with being a mother and father while he was gone, I didn't notice anything else. I missed the money coming out of the bank account unaccounted for and the late-night calls. I missed the random trips that came out of nowhere, and now I know they were for Tiffany's recitals. I missed it all. I was in a haze taking care of my children and our house. I thought I had it all. I thought I had won the lottery.

How do you accept that your husband has now had an affair? I could not sleep; I could not eat. I felt sick all the time. I no longer felt the love in my heart I once had being a mother. I felt betrayed and mislead and taken advantage of by the man I gave my life to. Here I was struggling to wake up in the morning with two little kids in the house, and he was in Chicago watching a dance recital. The sheer agony I felt was unbearable. My heart no longer felt whole. When I finally felt the strength to come clean to my family, I leaned on Rodney, my big brother, my savior.

Growing up, Rodney never let anyone mistreat me. We were inseparable as kids. He was my best friend. I never had to worry about a broken heart or ride to the mall as Rodney made sure I got whatever I wanted. He spoiled me so much that my momma used to say no man could compare. Well, no man, that was till I met Tony. Tony and Rodney hit it off right away. They both played football for our high school, and together, they made the team complete. They were always drinking together and laughing, fooling around like men do. The night I had to tell Rodney, I didn't know whose side he would take. I was nervous for the first time ever to talk to my brother. I knew how much he loved Tony! His reaction was all the same as it had been in years past. He gave me a hug and wiped my tears, and his first words were, "I'm gonna kill that bastard," but I told him no, I would figure it out and let me take care of it. He was always there for me, and this time, he would prevail like he always had. I cried night after night, imagining my husband running to the door to pick up his little girl. His brown-skinned little girl with a curly afro. I stopped being able to feel. I was numb all the time. The pain was a constant heartbreak I had to endure at every turn. I lost trust in my husband. I lost everything I knew and worked for and loved. I lost my family. I guess I could have walked away, got a divorce, prayed, and hoped for enough child support to survive, but I knew I wouldn't make it. I could not take seeing Tony with our kids and me not being there. I could not bear to see him married to another woman, living happily ever after. He was successful and had a career most would die for, and I had nothing. I had Tony, and I had Tony's income, and Tony's other kids! Not his first-born child but his later children. He was already accustomed to being a dad by then. I was the only one who was new to being a parent. I felt the hate creep up inside of me and dwell like a bad taste you can't get rid of, and I knew, I knew I wanted him to die. My rage was taking over my body, and just the look of him made me wish he were gone. I called Rodney late one night, and we planned the whole thing. It was easy since Rodney was a new detective and had inside information to crime scene analysis. I trusted him. I followed his every move to act as if I were working towards making things right. This was not an easy task. I had to pretend harder than ever. I had to be a woman I despised, the one who ran back to her cheating husband. I felt dirty. I felt like his touch made my stomach turn, and knots formed all over it. I played the game, though. I followed through on a romantic dinner to ensure I had an alibi. I was an all-or-nothing type of girl. I had committed, and that was it. After it was done, Rodney called me to confirm he was killed. He explained to me how he and my brother Ben beat him to a bloody pulp and then shot him. They left him for dead. It was an easy target because I made sure to get Tony drunk and then send him to the store. The rest I left up to Rodney. I did not need any more details. I just woke up empty. My husband was murdered. I made that happen, and I had to tell my kids their dad was dead. I had to pretend to be sad and cry for the news and media that poured in over a small-town murder. I got nervous, it got more attention than I anticipated, but Rodney told me to play cool and explained it would blow over. Oddly enough, he was right. In a few months, it was like no one even cared or remembered the name Tony Gray. I never heard from the whore he slept with or that illegitimate child he made. I just collected the life insurance through his job and drank away all the pain I never dealt with. The dark secret that lurked around every corner. I could not be a mother to my children. They reminded me of Tony. I could not stand the look on their faces when they cried for that monster. I wanted to tell them; I wanted them to hate him too. I was in a bubble, and nothing mattered anymore. Not my kids, not my life, not anything. I hate who I've become, and I know my kids will probably never forgive me or understand it, but I wrote them both letters. I explained everything in hopes of some empathy. I want to fix this and make things right. I am hoping to get off with lesser chargers and get out of here in time to meet my grandchildren. Should I ever have any. I have nothing but time now... Nothing but sober, quiet, time.

33

Tiffany

When Daniel and I got to Tampa, it was beautiful. The ocean was as blue as ever. I was in awe of this place. We booked our stay at the Sand Pearl Resort, and the view was breathtaking. I loved the sound of the ocean and the breeze that blew in our room. I sat on the balcony staring at the ginormous blue gem that was before me. Our first night was amazing. We ordered sushi by the pool and had lobster, and oh my God, it was the best way to satiate our taste buds. We enjoyed wine while walking on the beach with our toes in the sand, holding hands, and watching the sunset. I could not imagine a more beautiful, serene, peaceful moment. I took it all in, breathing the salty air and remembering my father. He was from here; he probably frequented this beach in his younger days. I imagined him running around the beach and jumping waves with his friends. I am sure he would have been a great dad to take beach trips with. I silently cried on the inside because I now have lost two fathers. For some reason, though, being here is only bringing back the memories of my birth father and all that he missed out on in my life. I squeezed Daniel's hand a little tighter and felt him squeeze back. I smiled. I loved this man. Once we were back at our hotel room, I decided to text Jerimiah.

"Hey, Jerimiah, it's Tiffany. Sorry for the late text. We got in safely, and we are settling in for the night. We are staying at the Sand Pearl. LMK if tomorrow works for you. We can meet for lunch. :)"

I wanted to ask Jerimiah so many questions about our dad, but I thought that might not be the best approach. I figured I would play it by ear. I was exhausted anyway, and sleep was the only thing on my mind. I got ready for bed and climbed in next to Daniel. I put my head on his chest, and that was the last thing I remember.

~

I am so nervous I cannot figure out what to wear. I was also nervous that today I might actually look more my ethnicity than most days. Ugh! My hair was never going to hold up in the humidity here, so I took the black girl approach. Now I am regretting it. I chose to get box braids and added the gold rings around my braids. I also chose to do a highlighted color which really makes me look a bit flashy. Daniel always reassures me I look beautiful, but what if Jerimiah takes one look and hates me? I realized this was real now, and I think before, I was just living in a fantasy of what might be but never actually come to be. Here I am, standing in my jean shorts with my very brown, tan legs showing, my red tank top, designer shades, and Tory Burch flip-flops. I grabbed my purse and filled it with my belongings. I took half my braids and put them up in a messy bun and left the bottom half down. This was it; I was going in as me. The real me. Daniel and I approached the diner First Watch and walked in looking for someone who resembles Jerimiah. As I looked around the room, I found a lot of white people and started to feel out of place. Daniel told me to breathe, but that was easier said than done. A hostess asked us how many? And I quickly told her four, but my voice was shaking. She led us over to a booth, and before I could sit down, someone tapped my shoulder. I turned around, and there was Jerimiah.

"Omigosh, girl, look at you, you are gorgeous! Hello, hello. Hunny, give me a hug. How are you? Omg, you must be Daniel. Hello, I am Jerimiah. It is so nice to meet you. Tiffany, you are absolutely stunning. I love your shades. You guys, this is Keith, my boyfriend. Say hi, boo."

I was in shock. He was nice. He was this loving, adorable skinny white boy with a handsome muscular Puerto Rican boyfriend, and they were just the cutest couple ever. I knew we were making waves in this area, a black girl from out of town and a gay white boy I am calling my brother with his gay lover.

"Clearly, we have the same taste in men," I said this very sarcastically, and everyone laughed. My Mexican man and his Puerto Rican man. Jerimiah sat right next to me and hugged me about a thousand times. We had a blast just talking and laughing and reminiscing on our past. He was so open and honest. He was warm and accepting. I loved every moment of being here with him, and I did not want this lunch to ever end. I was sad that Kayla chose not to come, but Jerimiah advised me he tried to reach out, but she has no interest in meeting me or ever coming back around. I was beyond words for how ecstatic I was meeting my brother that not meeting my sister was not a priority. I felt more fear in meeting her anyway. I just knew now that I had him in my life, I would never let him go. He would be my baby brother, whom I loved and adored from this day forward.

34

Kayla

I got my passport and changed my name at the courthouse. I am no longer going to associate myself with this town or these people. Slim had the nerve to send me a letter from her cell to try and apologize. I have no words for her. She disgusts me and can rot there for all I care. I was up late last night deciding where I was going to go trying to research different countries. I decided on Canada. First of all, they speak English, which is important to me since I literally speak only one language. I found a nice apartment in Alberta. I take pride in my white heritage, and it seems Canadians are the same. I found that there are several restaurants I could work for and then take online courses at University. I am going to move on in my life. Find a path and make friends. New friends. I am never coming back. I am going to fight for citizenship and enjoy a cold winter. Eat maple syrup and ride the trains. Embrace the new culture and start fresh. I will miss Jerimiah, but I can't face him and all he has become. I think more than anyone I will miss Niv, but she is on board with making changes. At this point, I view her as toxic. I can't be friends with someone who accepts gays and blacks. My family has tarnished our name. They have ruined my childhood, and all this coming to light has given me the answers to all my issues. I have to say the beach is my happy place, but it is filled with memories I would rather not revisit. Although I am starting over and leaving my hometown, I will be back to visit my father's grave. If he were here, he could explain to me his mistake with Seven and why he did what he did to our family. To me, to my mom and J. Without my dad, I have no reason to be here. I have no one to relate to or understand me. I am white. I wear my white skin proudly, and I will always be an American Girl. My life and my name changing. I will always remember where I am from and who I was, but in my future, I will never answer to the name Kayla Gray again. My roots may always be in Lutz, but my heart will now be in Canada.

www.ingramcontent.com/pod-product-compliance
Lightning Source LLC
Chambersburg PA
CBHW060040030426
42334CB00019B/2410